THE PUBLIC HOUSES OF HOUSES OF SUTTON COLDFIELD

1800 - 1914

Stephen Roberts

APS BOOKS

Yorkshire

APS Books,
The Stables, Field Lane,
Aberford,
West Yorkshire,
LE25 3AE

APS Books is a subsidiary of the
APS Publications imprint

www.andrewsparke.com

For Yvonne Moore

ACKNOWLEDGEMENTS

I am grateful to Kerry Osbourne who kindly volunteered to read my text before publication. My telling of these stories about the public houses of Sutton Coldfield has been greatly assisted by genealogical detail supplied by Yvonne Moore. She answered my queries with alacrity. Janet Jordan made me aware of a most useful unpublished essay.

Abigail Collingwood of Sutton Coldfield Library did not baulk at the list of public houses I submitted to her in the hope that there might be relevant photographs in its collections. All photographs in this book are reproduced courtesy of Sutton Coldfield Library. The two engravings are taken from the author's collection.

Andrew Sparke saw this book through the publication process.

CONTENTS

INTRODUCTION

In 1888 there were 46 premises in Sutton Coldfield that were licenced to sell alcohol. Of these 31 were fully licenced public houses and therefore able to sell beer, spirits and wine, five were beerhouses, six were off-licences selling only beer and four were off-licences selling beer, spirits and wine. Five years later there were 45 licensed victuallers and this figure hardly varied up to the First World War – there were 45 licenced houses in 1899, 47 in 1908 and 46 in 1913. That the number of public houses did not increase lay with the reluctance of the magistrates to approve new applications: they believed that there were already enough places to go drinking in Sutton.

Drinking in a tavern, 1846

'Drinking places', Brian Harrison has observed, 'existed for all types of customers.' [1] For gentlemen and travellers there were inns such

---

[1] B. Harrison, *Drinking Places & the Victorians: The Temperance Question in England 1815-1872* (Keele University Press, 1994), p. 45.

as the Three Tuns. There were also other public houses such as the Horse and Jockey and the Station Hotel that sought to present themselves as very respectable and offered accommodation. Working men were admitted – the publicans after all wanted their money - but there were separate rooms for different classes. Beerhouses were frequented by working people, where it was dry and warm and they often had their own chairs. Off-licences also catered for the working-class trade.

An inn was usually owned by a man of means – Harry Smith, who ran the Three Tuns for 45 years, also owned a substantial farm. Most public houses were run by working men, with the assistance of their wives and sometimes their adult children. They secured a licence from the magistrates whilst the leasehold and freehold were owned by others – in the later part of the nineteenth century these were often breweries. The public houses of Sutton were generally well-run and the renewal of licences went through without difficulty. It required repeated bad conduct for a licence not to be renewed: in 1877 it was reported that the licence of a 'house …near the Chester Road Station … was taken away on account of the misdeeds of the person who held it.' [2] For much of the nineteenth century many Sutton licensees also engaged in small-scale farming. Many public houses hosted auctions of houses, land and livestock. For the landlords the crowds that attended auctions would be sure to be in need of a pint or two of ale.

The working men who ran drinking places had to have certain skills – they needed, for example, to be able to keep accounts. A small number weren't suited to running a business or were too ambitious and their time as publicans ended in bankruptcy. They also needed to be physically strong men. Keeping a public house was an onerous way of life: it was not unusual for a landlord to have to eject a drunken man who refused to leave. It is little wonder that many licensees in Sutton moved on quickly. Only a small number of licensees of Sutton public houses remained in place for lengthy

---

² *Birmingham Daily Post,* 12 September 1877.

periods. When a licensee died, the magistrates usually approved the transfer of the licence to his widow. With a year or two, however, many of these were gone, but several women did continue as landladies for a number of years.

Until the later decades of the nineteenth century, the beer sold in public houses was mostly brewed on the premises. When a licensee left, it was common for brewing utensils to be listed amongst furniture and other items for auction. By the end of the nineteenth century Ansell's of Aston had a large stake in the supply of beer in Sutton. Thanks to the temperance movement, non-alcoholic drinks found their way into pubs, notably ginger beer and mineral water. Whilst the magistrates were prepared to issue licences for music and bagatelle, they did on occasion express their disapproval of dancing, a favourite activity of working people at holiday time.

Amongst those running an off-licence was a grocer at Wylde Green, Daniel Tilley. He supplied beer. In September 1886 he made his fourth appearance before the magistrates. He had been cautioned by the police against selling bottles of beer which were drunk immediately outside the shop. However, he carried on with this practice and was ordered to pay the costs in two cases and then fined 40s with costs in October 1885. [3] The question now was whether to renew his licence. The magistrates made the decision that they would, but Tilley was warned that it would not be renewed again if there were further complaints. In May 1898 he ceased to sell beer and his licence was transferred to Harriet Worrell.

The magistrates were often called on to consider applications for licences from shopkeepers. In general they were reluctant to grant these. Publicans were concerned by the competition – for example, when an off-licence was proposed near the King's Arms, the landlord declared that it 'would take half his trade away and was most "unfair, unjust and un-English." ' [4] In September 1887 an application was

---

[3] See ibid., 7 October 1885.
[4] *Birmingham Mail,* 7 February 1905.

received from Henry Wright, a grocer in Station Street. He was already in possession of a licence to sell beer and now sought a licence to sell wines and spirits. What Wright had in his favour was that he was a member of the town council and able to present in support of his application a petition which included the signatures of fellow councillors and churchwardens. What counted against him was that his shop was located close to thirteen licenced houses and there were two petitions, signed by 'the whole of the licensed victuallers … (and) a large number of inhabitants.' [5] The magistrates made clear their reservations, but granted the licence. Wright's son later disposed of the licenced part of the business and let part of his premises, known as no. 2, to a brewery, which was granted a licence, though the magistrates made clear that it was preferable for a licensee to live on the premises.

In 1899 there were six applications from shopkeepers to sell alcohol and one from a publican who wished to sell bottles of wine at his premises or to take out - but the magistrates granted only three licences. The applicants all employed legal representation. John Haynes wanted to sell beer at his small villa in Sheffield Road and, after being turned down the previous year, had erected a fence eight feet high at the rear and excavated a cellar at a cost of £40; his application was approved. Charles Dugmore, who ran the Central Stores in Boldmere, requested a licence for six days with an undertaking that his shop would be shut on Sundays. He was supported by a petition signed by 109 neighbours and the licence was granted. George Whitehouse of the Anvil Inn in Langley Heath was granted a wine licence.

The disappointed included George Adams, a baker and grocer trading from premises owned by his father on the corner of Holland Road whose barrister said that he was 'asked … almost daily for beer.' [6] To no avail his barrister had argued that the Cup 'was often in a very crowded condition and those persons who went for their

---

[5] *Warwickshire Herald,* 8 September 1887.
[6] Ibid., 31 August 1899.

beer had to pass in through the crowd standing about to get served
…' [7]

Those who were not granted licences often applied the following year. The most persistent applicant was George Chamberlain. He had moved from farming to running a grocery business with his wife in Mere Green, and applied for a licence on nine occasions. At his rejection in February 1908 he was informed that his application was not in order and his premises were unsuitable. 'It might save the applicant trouble and the Bench time if this was borne in mind in future years', the magistrates dryly observed. [8] Chamberlain returned with a new application the next year, his case being that he 'had been "implored" by a large number of residents to try and obtain a licence.' [9] It was put to him that 'it would save time if the counsel's speech were printed and simply handed up to the Bench year by year.' [10] A letter of opposition from the British Women's Temperance Association had been put in. 'These suffragettes always do object to everything', Chamberlain's solicitor observed. 'They are not suffragettes', he was informed 'and the ladies are just behind you.' [11] Chamberlain applied again in 1911 and 1913, but never gained the licence he sought. His son, Nelson Chamberlain, meanwhile, became the licensee of the Halfway House before his early death as the result of an accident whilst serving with the Royal Army Service Corps in France in 1917. [12]

As we have seen, most of the applications to sell alcohol were from shopkeepers. However, in October 1872, an application was received from Thomas Rea to convert a house he had built on a plot

---

[7] Ibid.,

[8] *Birmingham Mail,* 11 February 1908.

[9] Ibid., 9 March 1909.

[10] Ibid.

[11] Ibid.

[12] George Chamberlain died in 1944, aged 85, and became a resident of Sutton Coldfield Cemetery. The business he founded continued to thrive in Sutton Parade until the 1970s.

of land he had leased from the corporation into a public house. The building consisted of four rooms downstairs, a cellar and a clubroom, two bedrooms and outbuildings and was 'in every way a fit and proper house for a licence.' Rea had held a licence to sell spirits on the premises. He expected his new public house to be patronized by farm labourers and users of the railway station at Wylde Green. It was not unusual for such applications to be accompanied by a petition indicating local support – Rea managed to muster 84 signatures. Opponents to the proposal soon lined up. The Revd. Edward Kittoe of St. Michael's, Boldmere, pointed out that it was close to a corporation school and had been 'a serious nuisance to it' and that, when Rea had a wine licence, his house 'had been the resort of some of the worst characters.' [13] The police reported that they had been called to the house at 2 am to bring to an end a rowdy meeting of a women's benefit society. Unsurprisingly Rea's application was rejected.

For much of the nineteenth century drinking was the main recreation of working people. Ben Wilson has observed that it was 'so ingrained in British life because exertion was compensated by inebriation. It was not idleness that led to drinking but long and hard work.' [14] For the farm labourers who made up a large part of the population of Sutton drinking ale in the evening was their reward for the exhausting work they undertook - and besides there was little else to do. Standish Meacham has reported that 'a steady artisan might drink as much as two-quart pots of beer a day.' [15] Working class women had also become a much more visible presence in public houses by the end of the nineteenth century. Public houses were open from early morning until late evening on weekdays and for six hours on Sundays. It was not difficult therefore to get drunk – but this could lead to an appearance before the magistrates.

---

[13] *Birmingham Daily Post,* 1 October 1872.

[14] B. Wilson, *Decency & Disorder 1789-1837* (Faber & Faber, 2007), p. 75.

[15] S. Meacham *A Life Apart: The English Working Class 1890-1914* (Thames and Hudson, 1977), p. 124.

From the 1870s local newspapers carried lengthy reports of the Petty Sessions.   Let us look at a selection of the cases of drunken and disorderly behaviour that Sutton magistrates dealt with in these years. [16] With the opening of the railway lines into Sutton in 1862 and 1879, the men and women before the magistrates were as likely to be visitors to the town as those who lived there. The punishments meted out ranged from a caution to the payment of costs to the payment of a fine with costs. Previous offences and non-appearances only made the matter worse for the defendant.

In June 1871 William Jones, a labourer, was fined 40s with costs for assaulting a police officer at a public house during the Little Sutton Wake and 'behav(ing) in a most disgraceful manner, almost stripping himself.' [17]   In July 1886 Mary Ann Marshall was fined 11s 6d including costs after being summonsed and failing to attend court. In February 1887 Mary Bearman, a vagrant who was found drunk in Maney, was unable to pay the fine of 1s with costs and 'left Sutton by 2.10 train on route to Winson Green Gaol.' [18] In June 1887 Edward Hayman, a miller, was fined 2s 6d with costs of 12s 6d after assuring a police constable that he would return home with his horse and cart but instead 'called at the very next public house.' [19] In November 1887 Samuel Butler, a visitor from Manchester, was fined 2s 6d with costs after spending all day in a public house and then - in what the magistrates described as 'a very mean and abominable practice' - was turned out when he was drunk and his money had run out. [20] In June 1889 Patrick Dempsey, a recent arrival in the town, was issued with a caution after 'begg(ing) the Bench to let him off as he had a job of work to go to.' [21] In November 1894 Mary Robinson

---

[16] See also B.M. Milton 'Drink & the Mid-Victorians: A Study of Drunkenness in Sutton Coldfield 1877-1881' (1987). A copy of this typescript can be found on the website of the Sutton Coldfield Local History Research Group.

[17] *Aris's Birmingham Gazette,* 17 June 1871. A wake was a festival held annually.

[18] *Warwickshire Herald,* 10 February 1887.

[19] Ibid., 2 June 1887.

[20] Ibid., 3 November 1887.

[21] *Warwickshire Herald,* 22 June 1889.

was ordered to pay costs when she was found 'helpless … she fell down.' [22] In February 1900 Emma Hands was given a caution after being found drunk because she 'had some great trouble at home and she had come to Sutton to do something but did not know what.' [23] In February 1908 Annie Collins, a charwoman with thirty previous convictions, was remanded in custody for four days for throwing stones at the windows of the police station and wrecking her cell. In September 1913 George Smith was sentenced to three months with hard labour after kicking and biting a police constable 'like a raving madman.' [24] These personal stories testify to another important facet of life in Sutton during these years: there were lives lived with little hope of betterment.

We have statistics for the number of people who faced the magistrates for drunken and disorderly behaviour at the end of the nineteenth century and in the early twentieth century. In the year up to September 1888 70 people were proceeded against and in the year up to August 1889 107 were proceeded against; the police superintendent who presented this information declared this increase 'rather serious in a small place like Sutton.' [25] In the year up to August 1892 67 were proceeded against of whom 46 were convicted and 21 discharged on payment of costs or with a caution. In the year up to August 1893 80 were proceeded against with 46 convicted and 21 discharged. In the year up to August 1899 the figure stood at 131, one of these having already been convicted three times and another twice. It cannot really be said there was a pattern – the numbers went up and down almost at random. The figures remained at this sort of level in the early years of the twentieth century, but then began to fall significantly – in the year up to February 1903 37 were proceeded against (16 of them visitors), in 1909 28 (12 of them visitors) and in 1913 25 (including only one woman). What prompted increases in

---

[22] Ibid., 22 November 1894.

[23] *Harborne Herald,* 10 February 1900.

[24] *Birmingham Daily Gazette,* 3 September 1913.

[25] *Warwickshire Herald,* 29 August 1889. The figure for how many were actually convicted isn't provided in the report.

drunken and disorderly behaviour was not clear to the police or the magistrates; they always settled for the explanation that it was due to an increased number of visitors to the town.

A wife unsuccessfully tries to persuade her husband
to leave his favourite drinking place, 1895

In May 1863 a gathering of 2,000 temperance advocates took place in Aston Park. There were speeches, bands and generous supplies of tea, coffee and ginger beer. In the evening a hot air balloon took off and drifted towards Sutton. It was the nearest the temperance cause got to Sutton until the late 1870s. The advocates of temperance never really made much progress in Sutton. The Independent Order of Good Templars – which had strong roots in Birmingham - met in a room in Station Street and sought to focus on convincing children of the dangers of alcohol. When the United Kingdom Alliance – the most militant of the temperance organisations - called a meeting at the town hall in November 1877, fewer than 50 attended and half of those walked out when a resolution in favour of legislation which would give ratepayers powers to close public houses was put forward. [26] The local branch of the British Women's Temperance Association – a strongly-supported national organization - presented memorials to magistrates at licencing meetings and were often there in person. In December 1898 they successfully limited the extension of opening hours at Christmas in Sutton to just Boxing Day. They also organized talks and parties for children.

For temperance reformers the alternative to the public house was the coffee house. At a meeting at the town hall in summer 1878, with the rector W.K. Riland Bedford in the chair and many other chairs in front of him unoccupied, it was decided to open a Church of England-endorsed coffee house in Sutton and one duly appeared on Mill Street in December. [27] For 1d patrons could enjoy a cup of coffee, cocoa or tea. Upstairs there was a reading room. By 1880, however, the involvement of clergymen – which was thought to deter working men - in the venture was over and the North Warwickshire Coffee House Company was born. The coffee house in Sutton re-located to much larger premises in High Street and, in July 1880, expanded into Erdington. W.H. Tomes relaced a clergyman as manager. With a coffee room, a separate room for ladies, a smoking room, a bagatelle room and a chess room, it attracted many customers and was soon appealing to travellers with its 'well-aired beds.' [28]

---

[26] See B.M. Milton 'Drink & the Mid-Victorians' pp. 9-11.

[27] See *Birmingham and Aston Chronicle,* 24 June 1878.

[28] *Harborne Herald,* 23 July 1887. See B.M. Milton, 'Drink & the Mid-Victorians', pp. 11-17.

THE PUBLIC HOUSES OF SUTTON COLDFIELD 1800-1914

The Anvil

Located at Langley Heath on the rural east side of Sutton Coldfield, the Anvil appears to have been in business in the mid-nineteenth century. It was not unusual for farmers to run a beer house as an additional source of income at this time, and this appears to have been the case with the Anvil. It seems likely, however, that this beerhouse did not trade continuously in the second half of the nineteenth century. In 1890 John Lawrence was running the Anvil and a family member W.T. Lawrence had secured the licence for the Pilgrim Tavern in Great King Street in Birmingham. Together they advertised for a 'youth (strong) to do gardening; make himself useful; live in.' [29]

Public houses were permitted to provide alcohol during unauthorized hours to travellers who were three or more miles from home. A police constable visited the Anvil in November 1894 and arrested two men who were sharing a pint of beer and claiming to be travellers; they were in fact residents of Sutton and were fined 10s with 6s costs each for this deception. In November 1902 a bricklayer called Edward Griffiths was also arrested there. A resident of Berkswell, he had left his two children with an aunt from where they soon entered the workhouse. Having then tramped around the country, Griffiths found work at the Anvil. He was sentenced to three months with hard labour for abandoning his children. At this point the landlord was George Whitehouse, married without children and employing a servant.

During its early existence the main customers of the Anvil were mostly agricultural workers, but it became increasingly popular with

---

[29] *Birmingham Mail,* 27 January 1890. That year he also offered a trap and harness for sale.

cyclists. Whitehouse found himself being asked for claret and soda and hock and soda by cyclists and, in August 1899, successfully secured a licence to sell wine. His application was strengthened by the belief that wine was 'better for them than beer as it had a tendency to increase temperance.' [30] In March 1925, when the Birmingham cycling club the Ivy Wheelers called in for refreshments, this drinking place was styling itself the Anvil Hotel and in the possession of J.W. Hewett.

The Barley Mow

When William Bayliss, the farmer of a few acres in Hill, died in May 1827, he had also been landlord of the Barley Mow for almost thirty years. That summer all his livestock and agricultural implements - including two wagon mares which were 'known good workers', 'one famous milking cow', two sheep, carts, ploughs and harrows - were sold at auction. [31] It was the intention of his widow Mary to continue running the inn, but she abandoned the plan and, in May 1828, this 'old established, respectable and well-accustomed public house and premises' went up for sale by auction. The property was 'in complete and substantial repair', and came with stabling for twelve horses, a barn, piggery, large garden and five acres of 'rich pasture land.' [32] Bids were also invited for the furniture, brewing vessels and stock of ale 'which is very prime.' The inn was put up to let in May 1830, and the new landlord was Edward Lambley. He continued to benefit from travellers passing along the road through Hill, and increased his trade by permitting regular auctions of property, land, livestock and furniture at the tavern. However, trade slumped when a turnpike road opened through Mere Green. This old tavern did not close – it moved. The Barley Mow was now to be found in Mere Green, and its new landlord in 1859 was Thomas Cashmore. He had previously been employed as a coachman in Chorley and later ran an inn in

---

[30] *Warwickshire Herald*, 31 August 1899.
[31] *Aris's Birmingham Gazette*, 2 July 1827.
[32] Ibid., 12 May 1828.

Tenby.   In September 1878 this 'capital, old-licenced, roadside country inn' was put up for sale at a price of £500. [33]

It was common for inquests to be held in public houses in the nineteenth century.   When, in May 1895, William Thursfield died after being run over by a wagon and horses in Mere Green, the inquest was held two days later at the Barley Mow; the jury returned a verdict of accidental death.   At this time the Barley Mow was in hands of the Pindar family.   In May 1889 the licence passed from Charles Pindar to George Pindar.   John Pindar and his unmarried daughter Charlotte were also living at the inn.   When, in January 1893, two lambs broke through the hedge of the inn's garden, Charlotte Pindar sought damages; she only agreed to withdraw the case 'with some reluctance.' [34]

Mere Green, 1900 with the Barley Mow on the left

There were occasional outbreaks of violence. One evening in July 1895 James Swift, a grocer, struck John Brown whilst at the Barley Mow. Both men were turned out of the tavern. When the following evening Swift again assaulted Brown in the Four Oaks Tavern, he

[33] *Birmingham Daily Post,* 18 September 1878.
[34] *Warwickshire Herald,* 19 January 1893.

was fined 2s 6d with 2s 6d costs by the magistrates. In July 1892 John Pindar was assaulted by William Newbrook, a labourer, when he set up a target for his air gun in the yard of the New Road Tavern; Newbrook was fined 2s 6d.

With the departure of the Pindars, a Mr Clew became the licensee. When he died in 1896, his wife took over the licence. In 1910 a club room was added to the Barley Mow, paid for by Ansells. In 1913 a motor bus service was launched in Sutton; handily it was now possible to get on the bus at Chester Road tram service or Wylde Green Post Office or the Parade and get off at the last stop, the famous Barley Mow.

The Beggar's Bush

Also sometimes known in the nineteenth century as the Hawthorn Bush, this inn was 'situate in … splendid country … a great calling house … where business is thoroughly genuine.' [35] It was predicted that the tavern 'will rapidly grow in value and importance.' [36] In the early 1880s the Beggar's Bush had a brewhouse, stabling and a coach house and was set in two acres, with eight cottages, five of them newly built, bringing in an annual income of £139 11s. Pigs were kept by the landlord of the tavern.   About this time Alfred King – formerly of the Gold Cross in Dale End - held both the licence and the lease. He acquired the licence and lease of another public house in Birmingham and in 1885 decided to leave the Beggar's Bush but wished to retain the lease. His successor as licensee seems to have been John Short, but, in 1891, the licence was transferred to John Foden. King employed a barmaid called Sarah Kimber. Tragically, with no apparent reason, she hanged herself in her room in February 1887. She was just 25 years old.

April 1885 was not a good month for King. He was twice assaulted. In the first case the assault took place after he demanded a number of men paid for their beer. There was, however, to be no prosecution:

---

[35] *Aris's Birmingham Gazette,* 12 March 1877.
[36] *Birmingham Daily Post,* 31 August 1882.

a few days later one of these men was himself assaulted and at the Quarter Sessions at Warwick his attackers were each sentenced to nine months' hard labour. In the second case, in which King had also thrown punches but 'was carried out and Mrs King applied some brandy to his eye', another two men had also refused to pay for their beer. [37] King made clear that he did not want them punished severely. Both received fines of 5s with costs. These events doubtless made King even more desirous to leave the Beggar's Bush.

The Beggar's Bush, 1907

William May was another landlord at the Beggar's Bush who found customers all too ready to use their fists. When a number of men refused to leave in June 1906, he was 'knocked down … and severely injured about the head.' [38] The culprit was fined 10s with costs, with three other men who refused to leave fined £1 with costs.

---

[37] *Birmingham Suburban Times,* 25 April 1885.

[38] *Birmingham Daily Gazette,* 13 June 1906.

The Bell and Cuckoo

The Bell and Cuckoo was in existence at the beginning of the nineteenth century, and it is very likely that it was older than that. This beerhouse was situated in Boldmere, which was 'with the public a favourite spot, long known for its salubrity of air and aspect ...' [39] The house was made available to let, with three acres of land, in November 1827. In May 1847 a one third share in the house was put up for auction. The advertisement referred to a coach house, stabling, a piggery and a garden. That summer a man was found dead in a hovel behind the Bell and Cuckoo. Boldmere was a prime location for the building of houses and in the early 1870s this old public house closed when 'the bell lost its clapper and the cuckoo migrated on account of the land being purchased by a gentleman well known in the neighbourhood but who ... subsequently died.' [40]

The Boldmere Tavern

It was a long-standing practice that, when the owner of a public house sold up, the purchaser would bring in someone to keep the business going whilst he sought a new tenant. That is what happened when the Boldmere Tavern was sold in 1891 and John Turner was installed and began selling beer without a licence. Turner, who lived in Kings Heath, had filled in at several public houses before. The magistrates wanted the practice eradicated, but Turner pleaded guilty and the case was dismissed on the payment of costs of 7s. This came with a warning, however, that, if he re-offended, the punishment would be much more severe.

The Boldmere Tavern was situated on Chester Road, near Wylde Green railway station. The beer house was put up for sale in June 1878. A Mr Besant and Charlotte Phillips were amongst those who held the licence in the 1880s. In August 1885 Besant and his wife put on a dinner for James Humphries, a former resident of Sutton.

---

[39] *Aris's Birmingham Gazette,* 22 August 1825. St. Michael's Church became a near-neighbour of the Bell and Cuckoo in 1857.
[40] *Birmingham Daily Post,* 12 September 1877.

Twelve men were present, 'the *piece de resistance* being the hind quarters of a buck which Mr Humphries had shot during a recent visit to Eastnor Park, Herefordshire.' [41] Phillips could not make a go of it and, at the end of 1888, was summoned by the South Staffordshire Water Works for the non-payment of her water rates. That year there was also an unspecified nuisance at the house which the magistrates insisted was dealt with in fourteen days. Later licensees included Richard Maunder (who bred and sold pigs), William Price, Richard Clarke and Seymour Melhuish.

This beer house was not a stranger to drunken and disorderly behaviour. In January 1889 Elizabeth Salmon was twice ejected and ended up in Boldmere Road, 'very drunk with a crowd around her.' [42] She was fined 2d 6d with costs. In September 1893 Henry Lewis 'went into the inn and, because the landlord knowing his character refused to supply him with liquor, did much damage to the bar of the inn, pulling down the gas pipes and smashing everything he could lay his hands on.' [43] He also managed to throw a salt cellar at another customer which hit him in the eye, 'injuring him so severely that he was confined to his bed the next day.' [44] Lewis was fined 2s 6d with costs for his disorderly behaviour and 2s 6d with costs for assault.

The Boot

Boot Hill was an area made up of a farm, a small number of cottages occupied by farm labourers and an inn. For over twenty years from the early 1840s the landlord of the inn was Joseph James, whose principal trade was making boots and shoes. [45] James died at the age of 48 in May 1863, and his wife Elizabeth took over running the beerhouse. She was still there, with her adult children, in 1881 and her activities included farming. Soon afterwards Charles Forbes

---

[41] *Birmingham Suburban Times,* 1 August 1885.

[42] *Warwickshire Herald,* 26 January 1889.

[43] *Birmingham Daily Post,* 27 September 1893.

[44] Ibid.

[45] See schlhrg.org.uk/history-spot/107-articles-241-280/1660-boot-hill-boot-inn-268.html

became landlord; in January 1889 he organized a shooting match in which 'a fair attendance of sportsmen' demonstrated 'very indifferent' skills as they shot at eight dozen sparrows and three dozen pigeons. [46] In 1890 the licence was temporarily transferred from Forbes to James Page and then a month later temporarily transferred to William Slater. In fact Slater and his wife were to stay for some years. In March 1893 they held a supper for their friends and were 'received with no little enthusiasm'; unfortunately a few days later Slater's wife was knocked over by a cyclist in Birmingham, 'suffering very severely from her injuries.' [47] Slater supplemented his income by breeding pigs. In 1899 James Lea became landlord; he was also employed as gate keeper at the Chester Road entrance to Sutton Park. His licence only permitted him to sell beer which he supplemented with catering - but his annual income was under £300. In March 1908 he applied for a full licence, arguing that the Boot was the headquarters of three large clubs. His application was rejected.

The Cock

Only a few facts can be established about the Cock at Wishaw Green. We know the names of the landlords –such as John Sandon in the 1820s and Joseph Kelley in 1890s. In summer 1890 an enquiry was held at the inn after the strange death of Edward Fleming, who had travelled from Co. Mayo to get work at harvest time. He had acquired a new knife and accidentally cut deeply into his thigh. He died in five minutes because 'no one present knew what to do.' [48]

The inn was a popular destination for cycling clubs – such as Laurels Cycling Club of Birmingham, which prohibited racing. The landlord of the Cock H. Drinkwater became an honorary member in 1908.

---

[46] *Warwickshire Herald*, 17 January 1889.
[47] Ibid., 23 March 1893.
[48] *Birmingham Suburban Times*, 28 June 1890.

The Crown

In the early 1880s the landlord of the Crown in Four Oaks was William Granger. He placed an advertisement in a Birmingham newspaper to say that he had found a handsome sheep dog which, if not claimed in three days, he would sell to defray expenses. Later that decade the landlord was John Walker, who was assisted by his wife Mary. Like other publicans, he encouraged auctions of furniture and farm animals at the tavern. Three girls called at the tavern one Sunday morning in September 1886 to buy a bottle of stout for their mother who was unwell. In the circumstances the magistrates issued a nominal 1s fine with 1s costs. Walker asked customers who he was unsure about to leave. Two carters from Walsall Murill Gwilt and Richard Gwilt bought a pint which they drank in the tap room, but then refused to leave. With assistance, Walker forcibly removed the two men who, one customer reported, 'nearly strangled him and blackened his eye.' [49] For this behaviour the brothers were fined 19s 4d each, including costs. In November 1894 Joseph Shankey spent what he had acquired from begging in the area at the Crown; in a very drunken state, he was arrested and the magistrates sentenced him to 14 days hard labour. After Walker's death his wife acquired the licence, but in June 1898 it was temporarily transferred to Sidney Nicholls.

The Cup

The Cup was owned by the corporation of Sutton Coldfield. It dated back to the mid-eighteenth century, making it one of the earliest public houses in Sutton Coldfield. Its name was derived from the strong local interest in horse racing. The licensee for much of the first half of the nineteenth century was Thomas Brentnall. He was also a small farmer in Maney, renting land from Emmanuel College, Cambridge; in January 1825 he was able to sell at auction timber from the oak trees growing on it. Inn-keeping and farming clearly provided Brentnall with a good living because he owned a well-made

---

[49] *Harborne Herald,* 3 November 1888.

cart, which had steel shafts and axles removed from a gig, was painted green and emblazoned with his name and address. When, in May 1832, the cart was stolen from outbuildings at the Cup a reward of three guineas was offered for information leading to a conviction. Brentnall was a subscriber to the Sutton Coldfield Society for the Prosecution of Felons, which put up two guineas of this sum, with Brentnall himself adding another guinea. [50] Brentnall's customers were mostly working men and for those of them who wished to fish in Wyndley Pool he arranged a subscription list to share the cost of buying a licence from the corporation. His attempt to set up a bagatelle board without a licence in 1836, however, was thwarted: 'Mr Croxall informed against.' [51]

The Cup, c.1890

---

[50] S. Roberts *Glimpses into Sutton's Past Part I 1800-1850* (Stourbridge, 2020), p. 24 for the Sutton Coldfield Society for the Protection of Felons.
[51] schlhrg.org.uk/sarah-holbeche-diary.html?start=16. Edward Croxall Willoughby was a Sutton solicitor.

The Bunn family also lived at the Cup at this time; 19-year old Elizabeth Bunn died there in March 1821. Brentnall continued to hold the licence, but by the late 1830s the landlord was Edwin Bunn. He was a member of the Staffordshire Yeomanry. In October 1839 Bunn was presented with a silver snuff box for his 'spirited conduct' when four men, who were conveying a gentleman from Lichfield to Birmingham, stopped for refreshments and tried to the steal 'cash of a considerable amount' from their passenger. [52] Bunn's son George married Brentnall's daughter and became licensee of the Cup. Bunn advertised the inn as a welcome stopping place for visitors to the town from Birmingham, declaring that he provided 'a good family dinner at 1 pm' and 'tea and coffee at any hour.' [53] He even provided the times that coaches left and returned to Birmingham on Sundays. When dinners were held so that working men could mark family marriages of their employers 'on each occasion … the usual excellent catering of Mr Bunn, the worthy landlord of the inn, gave great satisfaction.' [54]

One night in April 1857 the Cup was broken into. When Bunn's servant Mary Caffrey went downstairs in the morning she 'found everything in a state of indescribable confusion … the thieves had broken their way all over the lower part of the premises, locks, bolts and bars had been forced open and cupboards and drawers ransacked.' [55] A good deal had been stolen - two gallons of rum in a stone bottle, a quart of brandy in a glass bottle, two bottles of sherry, two bottles of port, four bottles of porter, four boxes of cigars, two hams, a loaf of bread, and a large piece of beef, 'the bones of which were found "picked clean" on the Green at the rear of the house.' [56] A culprit was soon apprehended. He was Samson Maddox and he declared he had not entered the Cup. At the Assizes at Warwick in August 1857 it was claimed that he had been in possession of a bottle

---

[52] *Aris's Birmingham Gazette,* 9 December 1839.
[53] *Birmingham Journal,* 26 February 1848.
[54] Ibid., 11 July 1857.
[55] Ibid., 9 May 1857.
[56] Ibid.

of brandy from the Cup and he was sentenced to ten years' transportation.

George Bunn succumbed to bronchitis in June 1860 aged 72. His successor was 25-year old Alfred Sheppard who was welcomed at a dinner, attended by fifty gentlemen, in August 1860. The dinner began at 4 pm and continued all evening, with toasts and songs. Rather usefully, his brother drove the omnibus from Birmingham to Sutton. [57] Sheppard continued to provide dinners for working men paid for by their employers – such as by Edelston & Williams in September 1862 – but did not remain long. The new licensee was Joseph Clibbery, who ran the inn with his wife Sarah. In September 1875 he agreed to the pitching of a tent capable of accommodating 500 people on land attached to the inn so that a picnic could be held for the costermongers and greengrocers of Birmingham.

At the end of the nineteenth century John Ellery held the licence for the Cup. When he died, his wife Mary managed the tavern into the early years of the twentieth century. As an attraction Ellery placed in the garden of the tavern in July 1886 a three hundredweight cast iron press once used by a notorious maker of counterfeit coins from Great Barr. Ellery was clearly a strong-willed man. He refused to pay the annual dole of 6s to the churchwardens that Thomas Brentnall had agreed to half a century earlier. If a party of sober men entered the inn accompanied by one drunken man, he declined to serve them. In April 1889 six young men arrived at the Cup and proceeded to throw the clock, railway timetables and almanacks on the fire, as well as spilling beer and scattering matches across the floor. They then visited the Duke and threw the clock there on the fire. They were fined between them 17s 3d including damages with costs for the first offence and 16s 5d for the second. In December

---

[57] In the census of 1861 Sheppard describes himself as 'victualler, guardian of the omnibus.' Married to Eliza and with one son, he employed two servants and an ostler to look after the horses of those who visited the tavern.

1896 John Kelly used 'very filthy' language when he was ejected for being drunk. [58] Unable to pay the fine, he spent 14 days in prison

By the early 1890s the Cup was an 'ancient but rapidly decaying business.' With 'a portion of it in an insecure state', Mary Ellery declared that rebuilding was 'absolutely necessary.' Ellery entered into a covenant to rebuild the inn at a cost of not less than £1,500 by the end of 1895. The old tavern would be demolished and a new building erected 'of a more commodious character in half-timber early English style'; there would be bar, tap room, kitchen, larder, bedrooms and a stable. [59] Ellery had an exemplary record as licensee and no complaint had ever been made against her. The town council, which owned the site and the building, and the magistrates readily agreed.

The Dog-In-The-Hole

Referred to locally as the Old Dog, this inn was, in the mid-nineteenth century, said to be situated 'at the entrance of the town of Sutton from Birmingham' - later known as Lower Parade. [60] We know something about the building at this time because it was put up for auction in January 1862 by its owner, George F. Ryman who intended to concentrate on his farm at Great Barr. The Old Dog consisted of a bar, tap room, club room and five bedrooms; at the rear was a brew house, two stables, a cow house, three piggeries and a blacksmith's shop occupied by John Ferneyhough. In an adjoining house, Ryman's daughter ran a grocery shop. With the inn sold, Ryman held another auction to sell his furniture, brewing utensils, hops, bacon, pigs and a 'barren cow.' [61]

In 1879 John Barton became the licensee and remained at the Old Dog for a decade. He was succeeded by William Crowley – who employed two servants and an ostler - and then, in 1891, by Thomas

---

[58] *Warwickshire Herald,* 3 December 1896.

[59] Ibid., 4 January 1894.

[60] *Aris's Birmingham Gazette,* 4 January 1862.

[61] Ibid., 22 March 1862.

Good. His father Samuel had been the landlord of the Star Liquor
Vaults and Tavern in Dale End. Betting was prohibited in public
houses and so Good ensured that, when he took bets on horses, he
did so immediately outside his public house; when he came before
the magistrates in June 1891, he was acquitted but told that he 'had
been encouraging betting but (they) hoped he would not continue it.'
[62] In July 1892 Samuel Coley, an ironfounder who had arrived in
Sutton from Walsall with a friend in a horse and trap, became
involved in an argument at the Three Tuns about being short-changed
before entering the Old Dog. Good would serve him only soda water
and Coley declared that he 'was not drunk but a little excited over
the bother.' [63] The magistrates were not persuaded by his defence
and fined him 5s with 14s 6d costs. Good has entered the business
with great hopes, but they clearly weren't realized because in
February 1893 the licence was transferred to John Grieg.

The Dog-In-The-Hole, c.1890

---

[62] *Birmingham Daily Post,* 24 June 1891.
[63] *Warwickshire Herald,* 21 July 1892.

A period of instability followed. Grieg had no plans to stay long and within a few months Eliza Leigh was the licensee. Her exit quickly followed with George Mainsford arriving. In April 1895 the licensee was Frank Wakefield, and a regular John Lilly was arrested for being in possession of an unopened packet of 24 counterfeit half crowns and 20 counterfeit florins. Lilly's solicitor argued that he was a respectable, hard-working man, that no counterfeit coins were found when his house in Erdington was searched and that he was unaware of the contents of the packet. Nevertheless the magistrates still decided to send him to the Quarter Sessions that would meet at Warwick that July. Lilly was acquitted, though with a stinging rebuke from the judge who informed him that he was 'a fool as no man in his senses would have acted as he had done.' [64]

In February 1896 the Old Dog was sold to John Thomson. Before the end of the century there had been two more licensees – Franklin Fisher, who was fined £5 with costs for permitting drunkenness on the premises - and Joshua Mortiboys. In 1902 Thomas Haughton was being employed as manager. The Sutton and District League, which arranged football matches, made the Old Dog their headquarters, as did the Sutton and District Air Rifle League. When the First World War broke out, Thomas Cunningham was the licensee. In July 1913 Cornelius Casey arrived at the Old Dog fresh from the police cells after assaulting a gate keeper at Sutton Park. Though the inn was not open, he could be served if he had travelled three miles or more and Casey truthfully informed Cunningham that he lived in Saltley. Before the magistrates, Casey declared that his main purpose in entering the house was to buy a sandwich – though he had ordered a pint of beer. He was fined 5s.

By 1914 there was a consensus that the Old Dog needed not alterations, but to be pulled down and entirely rebuilt.

---

[64] Ibid., 11 July 1895.

The Duke

During the nineteenth century Sutton was well-known as a centre for horse racing. The town even produced an illustrious jockey, John Wells, who on three occasions rode the winning horse in the Derby. It was Wells who, in 1853, had a house built in Sadler Street in Maney – named after the owner of the land, local solicitor Richard Sadler – which was to become the Old Duke Inn. [65] Opposite Wells' house an inn was erected which was given the name the Old Duke, in tribute to the Duke of Wellington who had died in 1852. The first landlord of this public house was Charles Atkins, who was also in trade as a grocer. In due course Sadler Street became known as Duke Street.

Wells' house offered more commodious accommodation for a tavern, and in 1866 Atkins transferred his business across the road. With a full licence, he was able to sell beer, spirits and wine. Auctions of livestock and furniture attracted large crowds and increased trade and he always seemed to have horses to sell. In 1876 he offered a bay gelding, a 'good goer ... perfectly quiet and sold for no fault', and a black cob gelding, 'thick set, good action, suit heavy gentleman to ride'; in 1877 it was a bay pony, 'remarkably handsome ... a good goer'; and in 1878 it was three bay geldings 'suitable for carriage or trade, sound, quiet, no vices.' [66] These horses were kept in the extensive stables of the Duke; when a brown pony strayed in November 1870, Atkins offered a reward. Atkins' hopes that a 'capital, strong' spring cart might go quickly in 1864 were not realized; he had to re-advertise it as 'a bargain', doubtless having reduced the price.[67] Early in 1877 Atkins decided to make some

---

[65] For a full history of the Duke by Yvonne Moore see midlandspubs.co.uk/warwickshire/sutton-coldfield/duke-inn.htm
[66] *Aris's Birmingham Gazette,* 8 April, 15 July 1876; *Birmingham Daily Post,* 23 March 1877, 22 July 1878.
[67] Ibid., 13 June 1864, 13 May 1865.

improvements to the Duke; he advertised for carpenters, 'liberal wages paid, fare paid.' [68]

When Atkins died in 1880, his widow Eliza took over the business. The Duke continued to thrive, and mineral water, produced in the tavern's outbuildings by Thomas Read, was soon on sale [69] In May 1882 Eliza Atkins found herself in court. Her son sent bailiffs to the house of John Aspinall, also a licensed victualler, in Green Lanes, whose son owed her money. The bailiffs removed a milch cow. The cow was returned after three days, and Aspinall agreed to pay £3 3s.

A series of temporary tenants followed, one of whom, Emily Richards, was declared bankrupt in August 1884. She did not appear at the hearing. In February 1885, the Duke was put up for sale – but this did not go through. It seems that, in 1897, Eliza Atkins sold the Duke to the Holt Brewery Company. [70] She was sufficiently well-off to be able to send the years until her death in March 1913 in Anchorage Road. The new owners added a tap room, and John Harrison, formerly of the Queen's Head in Birmingham, secured the licence and the lease. The Duke was heavily promoted in the newspapers and became the headquarters of Royal Sutton Coldfield Cycling Club, Sutton Coldfield Football Club and Maney Cricket Club. With the departure of the mineral water manufacturer Thomas Read to a purpose-built factory on the corner of Lower Queen Street and Upper Holland Road, Harrison sought to attract a new tenant, emphasizing the tavern's 'splendid artesian well and abundant supply of water.' [71] He also supplemented his income by taking in horses at the stables. Harrison died at the Duke in March 1906.

The Duke now seems to have been in the hands of the mineral water manufacturer John Thompson, with the owners of the freehold still

---

[68] *Birmingham Mail,* 14 February 1877.

[69] S. Roberts' *Glimpses into Sutton's Past Part III 1886-1914* (Stourbridge, 2021) p.3 for Read's business.

[70] See *Birmingham Mail,* 12 February 1891, 21 February 1901 for this very successful brewery.

[71] *Birmingham Daily Post,* 9 April 1900.

being the Holt Brewery Company. Harrison may have taken over the buildings vacated by Thomas Read. Certainly it was Thompson, with the assistance of the Birmingham auctioneers Gray & Walker, who negotiated the sale of the tavern to Charles Williams. He asked for for £500, Williams offering £300 and then eventually paying £482 10s on condition 'that the question of dilapidation was settled with the Holt Brewery Company.' [72] In 1912 the magistrates refused to approve a licence until alterations had been completed and the tavern was not open for business.

There were a number of incidents of customers being drunk at the Duke. Like the majority of Sutton public houses, it was well- run, with licensees taking no risks of losing their licences by failing to come down firmly on drunkenness. Those who refused to leave were escorted out by a police constable and fined 2s 6d with costs by the magistrates – as John Wood and George Bragg discovered in 1891 and 1895 respectively. In summer 1910 a fight broke out on the premises between two labourers from Sutton, Thomas Carwell and Edwin Goodwin; they were both fined 5s including costs.

The Emmanuel College Arms

Emmanuel College, Cambridge, owned a considerable amount of land across Sutton. The rents it received from its tenants were an important source of income for the college.[73] The Emmanuel College Arms stood at the top of Mill Street on the site of a 17th century inn called the Bull's Head. This building had been demolished in the 1760s and replaced by a new inn which was originally called the Sun. [74] In the early part of the nineteenth century the licensee was Robert Betts who, after his death, was succeeded by his wife Martha, who

---

[72] *Birmingham Mail,* 13 May 1910. When Gray and Walker retained £15 7s 6d for their part in the sale, Thompson unsuccessfully sued them.

[73] See schlhrg.org.uk/history-spot/111-articles-401-440/1816-college-estate-arms-439.html

[74] See sclhrg.org.uk/history-spot/108-articles-281-320/1703-emmanuel-college-arms-283.html

died in April 1866. The inn became known as the College Arms in the mid-nineteenth century.

The College Arms was frequently made use of by Sutton's auctioneer Samuel Kempson. Large crowds gathered to bid for houses, land and plantations of young trees. Later in the nineteenth century Sutton's redundant gasworks were sold off at the College Arms. The inn was also used for meetings and dinners. The Sutton Coldfield Protection Society, established in 1854, to challenge the authority of the corporation met there, as did a local committee to return a Liberal MP for North Warwickshire in 1874.[75] In November 1885 the Sutton Coldfield and District Club was formed at the College Arms. Its first objective was - from September to March each year - 'to destroy sparrows.' [76] These birds were disliked because they damaged crops; it was agreed that 4d per dozen would be paid for the heads of sparrows. The annual subscription to join the club was 1s with an additional 6d for every additional twenty acres of land. The second objective of the club was to secure a reduction in tithe payments; it was agreed to send a deputation to meet the rector, W.K. Riland Bedford.

Members of clubs looked forward to their annual dinners, which lasted into the early hours. A favoured venue was the College Arms where the dinners were 'of a substantial character and being very well cooked and served fully maintained the reputation of Mrs Green … as a caterer.' [77] Amongst the satisfied customers were the Piscatorial Society, the cricket club and one of the football clubs. [78] Elizabeth Green had taken over the licence after the death of her husband Robert Green in January 1888. His father owned saw mills in Birmingham, but he had become a publican in that town. He held

---

[75] For the Sutton Coldfield Protection Society see S. Roberts *Glimpses into Sutton's Past Part II 1851-1885* (Stourbridge, 2021), pp. 15-17.

[76] *Warwickshire Herald,* 19 November 1885.

[77] Ibid., 19 January 1893. Robert Green is listed as the licensee in 1871.

[78] For the Piscatorial Society see S. Roberts, *Glimpses into Sutton's Past Part III* (Stourbridge, 2021), p. 62.

the licence for the Red Lion in Lancaster Street before moving to Sutton in 1866. He built up a reputation in the town as an honest, genial man and the heyday of the College Arms was the thirty years when it was run by the Greens.

Mostly there was little disorder, but in June 1889 a police constable was called to the inn when a fight broke out. John Dolan was the instigator, and broke a number of jugs and glasses. He paid for this damage, but was also fined 5s with costs by the magistrates. When beggars entered the inn, a police constable was called and the next morning they were before the magistrates. The punishment was usually 14 days' hard labour. The magistrates believed that these men and women were feckless and too idle to work and that begging could only be eradicated by doling out harsh punishments.

After Elizabeth Green left the College Arms in February 1898, it went into decline. No public house in the town had fewer customers. In nine years, the licence was transferred eight times. The brewers Frederick Smith Ltd of Aston, who held the lease from Emmanuel College, briefly took over in an attempt to improve the situation, but the licence was soon being transferred from one landlord to another, amongst them John Witts – fined £5 and costs for permitting betting on the premises in November 1898 - John Grainger and Samuel Taylor. The height of the rooms ranged from 7' 8" to 8' 6" which did not meet the legal requirement of at least 9'. The police expressed concern that it was difficult to supervise the premises because they were not self-contained, with free access at the rear to a butcher's yard and to Mill Street. In 1907 the magistrates refused to renew the licence. The College Arms was 'dilapidated' and 'a redundant tavern' and was demolished with a new Post Office opening on the site at the end of 1909. [79]

---

[79] *Birmingham Mail,* 11 February 1908, *Birmingham Daily Gazette,* 12 February 1908.

The Fox

Auctions, a common occurrence at many public houses in nineteenth century Sutton, were not held very often at the Fox – though, in July 1852, Sutton's leading auctioneer Samuel Kempson was there to sell land and houses; one cottage had the attraction a 'well of excellent water.' [80]

However, it didn't miss out on outbreaks of drunken and brutal behaviour. In September 1869 Thomas Barlow and Thomas McHugh, having spent an evening drinking together at the inn, became embroiled in a very violent quarrel in which a knife was drawn and a stone used as a weapon. Barlow was acquitted, having successful argued that McHugh had provoked the quarrel and that he had acted in self defence. In June 1885 William Chilwell, a labourer, became drunk and refused to leave the inn; his case had to be adjourned by the magistrates because he was 'in the General Hospital, Birmingham, suffering from a broken leg caused at the time that he was ejected from the house by the police.' [81] In January 1904 there was 'a wrangle in the kitchen' at the Fox; Edward Rhodes accused Joseph Woodward, a gamekeeper at Penns Hall, of reporting him for setting traps and then 'struck him a blow in the eye, cutting it very badly' for which he was fined 5s with 14s 6d costs.

When a public meeting was called in Walmley, the Fox was the obvious venue. There was a meeting in February 1867 concerning the state of the roads which 'were managed disgracefully'; it was resolved to lobby the highways committee of the corporation. [82] The Sutton Coldfield Workmen's Association was formed to ensure the interests of working people were raised during elections to the town council and sought to establish branches in every ward; in March 1886 25 men came together to form such a branch at the Fox, with Thomas Birtles as secretary. Inquests were also held at the inn – such

---

[80] *Aris's Birmingham Gazette,* 5 July 1852.
[81] *Birmingham Suburban Times,* 20 June 1885.
[82] *Aris's Birmingham Gazette,* 22 February 1867.

as that concerning the death of John Burton who died walking to his lodgings and whose sister described him as 'not a very sober man … he was fond of a drop of beer.' [83]

In the 1860s the licensee was John Weldon. Each year he held what he called an anniversary dinner – perhaps to mark his acquisition of the licence – and charged 1s 6d for tickets. He died in Walmley in March 1887, aged 83. Before this his wife Eliza – known as Betsy - had acquired the licence.   In October 1884 she faced a charge of selling alcohol on a Sunday. The case was dismissed when it was accepted that John Parry, the man to whom she had provided a jug of beer, was 'an intimate friend of Mrs Weldon's for many years and was in the habit of visiting her house very frequently.' [84]   The magistrates declared that 'they could not conceive a number of respectable persons coming forward and telling a direct lie.' [85]   The following year she gave up the licence. In the 1890s John Clifford became the landlord. He was keen to bring in more catering trade; in 1908 Christmas in Walmley was celebrated at the Fox with Ye Olde Village Feast.

The Fox and Dogs

By the nineteenth century the Fox and Dogs had been in existence for well over a hundred years. In the eighteenth century the landlords included Samuel Smith and William Lambley. [86] One of the earliest references in a newspaper to a public house in Sutton is to the Fox and Dogs – in May 1809 an auction of two local houses with gardens was held there. Up until the end of the nineteenth century we find regular newspaper advertisements for auctions at the tavern for houses, furniture, land and livestock.

---

[83] *Warwickshire Herald,* 24 June 1886. Burton was recorded as having died of a haemorrhage of the lungs.
[84] Ibid., 25 October 1884.
[85] *Birmingham Daily Post,* 22 October 1884.
[86] See sclhrg.org.uk/history-spot/138-articles-481-500/2223-fox-and-dogs=490.html

The landlord of the Fox and Dogs in the 1840s was William Marler, who also farmed fifty acres of adjacent meadow and arable land. At this point the tavern had five bedrooms. After Marler's death, his wife carried on the business. When she died in 1855, the tavern became available to let. It was described as an 'old-established and well-accustomed inn … by the side of the road leading from Walsall etc to Tamworth and Fazeley.' [87]   The 'excellent live and dead farming stock, household furniture and tavern effects' were auctioned off.[88]

In winter 1865-6 the Fox and Dogs was again available. The tavern came with outbuildings such as a barn and stable and a 'capital garden'.   [89] The land attached to the tavern was divided up into separate lots. Samuel Langley was the landlord at this time, but in December 1868 he decided to leave. He sold at auction twelve ale casks which held from 40 to 110 gallons, jugs and glasses, cutlery, furniture and a pianoforte. His involvement in farming is evident from the other items he sold at auction, including wagons, carts, a plough, harrows, a rick sheet, a turnip pulper, a straw cutter, pig troughs and a wheelbarrow. Charles Lloyd was briefly landlord until the arrival of William Burton in 1871; he was to remain at the Fox and Dogs, with his family and employing one servant, until 1889. Burton gave up Hill Wood Farm to concentrate on the tavern, though he did make use of the farm buildings on the site. In August 1884 these were destroyed in a fire. At one point the tavern itself was in jeopardy, but was saved when a large number of local men rushed to the scene. The damage amounted to £300 – fortunately Burton had taken out insurance. The following year Burton sold all his livestock of 45 sheep, six cows and an unspecified number of pigs,

---

[87] *Birmingham Journal,* 10 March 1855.
[88] *Aris's Birmingham Gazette,* 5 March, 26 March 1855. The furniture included mahogany and oak dining tables and chairs and drinking tables and the tavern utensils included brewing vessels 'well-seasoned ale casks' and an 'ale machine'
[89] *Birmingham Daily Gazette,* 18 January 1866.

The police constables viewed the Fox and Dogs as being a badly-run house. In September 1873 Superintendent Galloway opposed the renewal of Burton's licence – but he did manage to retain it. There was a confrontation between Burton and two police officers in plain clothes in October 1874. They claimed that Burton was trading during unlawful hours. Burton became 'very abusive, demanding their names and saying they might be thieves for all he knew.' [90] His defence was that he had served ale to four lodgers and five cattle dealers from West Bromwich who had arranged to stay the night. To the chagrin of the police, the case was dismissed.

There were, however, only a small number of incidents at the Fox and Dogs during Burton's tenure that were to result in appearances before the magistrates. William Mason, a local brass polisher, who was 'in the habit of calling just to look around' was fined £1 with costs for being drunk in March 1888; the magistrates imposed a small fine because it was his first offence and he was being treated for epilepsy. [91] 'Blood was flowing freely and glasses and bottles were flying all about the room' when, during an election to the town council in November 1886, two men exchanged blows; they were each fined 10s 6d with costs. [92]

John Ordish succeeded Burton as landlord. He also bred and sold boars at 2s 6d each. The Hill Friendly Society, founded in 1846, held its meetings and dinners at the Fox and Dogs; in March 1885 they arranged a fair in the gardens of the inn, with sports, roundabouts, pole climbing for a leg of mutton and dancing on the lawn. It was a longstanding rule of the society that its silk hat bands and silk scarves were kept in the clubhouse under the care of the landlord. After Ordish left the Fox and Dogs in January 1891, the society discovered that he had not handed over these items to the new landlord. Ordish

---

[90] *Birmingham Daily Post,* 13 September 1873.

[91] *Warwickshire Herald,* 22 March 1888.

[92] *Birmingham Suburban Times,* 18 November 1886. In the election the sitting councillor was returned by 141 votes to 95. Ibid., 6 November 1886: ' ... but for a squabble in a public house in the neighbourhood of the polling booth, everything would have passed off very quietly.'

claimed they had been left in a cupboard. A search of the inn failed to find the missing items. Ordish eventually agreed to pay £5 in monthly instalments of 5s to cover the cost of the missing items, but failed to make any payments. Ordish now found himself in court, but his solicitor argued that he had only withheld the items and had not committed fraud. The magistrates dismissed the case.

The landlord of the Fox and Dogs in the 1890s and 1900s was John Plant. In 1892 he refused to sell beer to James Beck 'and from that time he had been a continual nuisance to him.' [93] When he insulted a female servant and threatened to start a fight in April 1893, he was fined 2s 6d with costs. In 1895 Charles Forester engaged a bed for the night, went out and came back intoxicated and, unable to get in, kicked and damaged the door; unable to pay the fine of £1 1s, he was sent to the gaol at Warwick for fourteen days.

The Gate

When the Gate in Mill Street was put up for auction in July 1858 it was described as a 'capital old-established house' occupied for many years by Walter Wilmore. It was stated that visitors to Sutton Park provided the Gate with 'a large trade.' [94] Wilmore was succeeded as landlord by Walter Cashmore and then by William Coaley. He used French millstones to grind barley and wheat which he used to brew his beer. In 1865 these were for sale - 'a bargain – to be sold, cheap a pair of French millstones … ready for work.' [95] With Coaley dead, the Gate became available to let with 'licence, goodwill, possession etc' [96]

In 1880 Thomas Thomas acquired the licence. He employed two servants. Twice he found himself before the magistrates accused of being drunk on his own premises – a licensee could only be prosecuted if the public house was open when he was suspected of

---

[93] *Warwickshire Herald,* 13 April 1893.
[94] *Birmingham Daily Post,* 5 July 1858.
[95] Ibid., 27 April 1865.
[96] *Birmingham Daily Gazette,* 25 March 1869.

being drunk. In March 1885 a police constable declared that, when he entered the Gate, Thomas' speech was 'not coherent' and he was clearly drunk. [97] Thomas stated that he was quietly reading a book. His solicitor Joseph Ansell, who defended all the brewery's licensees when they found themselves in court, argued that there had been no disturbance. In light of this, the magistrates decided not to impose a fine. In February 1886, however, Thomas was convicted of the offence and fined 10s 6d with costs.

Mill Street with the Gate on the left

At this time Mary Dorillan was employed as a kitchen maid at the Gate. She was accused of stealing three pairs of boots. The boots were 'old and mouldy and thrown on one side and were in fact such as were considered by servants as perquisites.' The boots were returned and Thomas' wife 'freely forgave her' but Dorillan wasn't going to be allowed to get away with it. The magistrates fined her 10s with 23s costs.[98] The boots were worth 5s.

During the 1890s Albert Bladon was the licensee. Married with children, he employed three servants, two of whom worked in the

---

[97] *Warwickshire Herald,* 28 March 1885.
[98] Ibid, 2 May 1885.

inn. When alterations were being made to the premises in autumn 1890, John Farmer, a bricklayer's labourer, entered the cellar and removed a pint of brandy, a pint of ale and half a pint of stout, worth 4s 6d. He was found in the yard 'helplessly drunk', but Bladon asked for leniency. [99] The magistrates interpreted leniency as imprisonment for one month. There was a disturbance at the Gate in summer 1907 in which John Smith, a polisher, hit Frederick Whitby, a clerk, on the head with a jug; he was fined 50s with costs. This was an unusual occurrence – Sutton Town, a very respectable football club, held their committee meetings at the Gate.[100]

The Gate (Boldmere)

In spring 1869 the Gate at New Oscott, described as an 'old-licenced road-side house' was put up for sale at an asking price of £120. [101] In March 1882 it was again for sale 'through illness'; it was presented as a 'rare chance for a cow keeper.' [102] With a full licence, it could sell beer, spirits and wine. The licensee from the time of this sale until his death in 1894 was Henry Mee, known for his 'genial and happy disposition.' [103] Agents for Ansells in Sutton and Aston, Henry Mee & Sons, could supply 36 gallons of ale for 42s. On its creation in 1886, Mee was elected to Sutton town council, and delegated the running of the inn to a manager Alfred Coley, known to all as Bertie. Mee was a Conservative but 'fearless and outspoken' in speaking up for the poor. [104] Coley succeeded Mee as licensee, but died only four years later in 1898.

Auctions of local property were often held at this tavern – for example, in March 1878, the three-bedroom house in Highbridge Road of the late Thomas Garland with 'brick-built cow house,

---

[99] *Birmingham Daily Post,* 24 September 1890.
[100] S. Roberts, *Glimpses into Sutton's Past Part III 1886-1914* pp. 59-60 for Sutton Town.
[101] *Birmingham Daily Post,* 7 May 1869.
[102] Ibid., 16 March 1882.
[103] *Warwickshire Herald,* 16 August 1894.
[104] Ibid., 16 August 1894.

piggeries, chaff house and … a very large garden, fully planted with fruit trees.' [105] Smoking concerts and dinners were regularly held at the Gate. In winter 1884-5 a series of smoking concerts featuring 'some special and good talent' took place. [106] In May 1885 thirty employees of the Universal Fire Arm Works gathered to celebrate the coming of age of the youngest son of their employer Robert Hughes. In October 1892 the annual dinner of the New Oscott Golf Club was held at the Gate, drawing to a close at midnight with singing of the national anthem.

The most alarming criminal offence which took place at the Gate occurred in December 1885 when a group of men assaulted a plain clothes police officer. When they were refused drink, the officer was 'attacked with sticks, besides being brutally kicked.' [107] Nine men faced hefty fines of between 20s with costs and 40s with costs. In November 1896 Francis Jacobs, a hawker, was sentenced to one month with hard labour for stealing a coat. In August 1899 William Adams and Thomas Adams were fined £1 for pretending to be travellers; 'this sort of thing must be stopped in Sutton', observed one of the magistrates. [108]

And then there was Kate Capewell, a former licensee of the Gate. Standing outside the inn in 1904, she heard Thomas Lewis refer to 'her fancy man Webb.' [109] She took the surprising step of suing him for slander. The jury returned a verdict for Lewis.

The Greyhound

William Hodgetts became licensee of the Greyhound in 1850; he was succeeded by his son Joshua Hodgetts and then briefly by his grandson Joshua Jesson Hodgetts. Situated near to Oscott College, the Greyhound had a garden and was adjoined by a few acres of

---

[105] *Birmingham Daily Post,* 2 March 1878.
[106] *Warwickshire Herald,* 23 May 1885.
[107] *Birmingham Mail,* 2 December 1885.
[108] *Warwickshire Herald,* 24 August 1899.
[109] *Birmingham Mail,* 14 December 1904.

arable land and four cottages. William Hodgetts and his son were both farmers. In September 1869 William Hodgetts offered a reward when four of his heifers, each marked with his initials on one of their horns, strayed or were stolen from Sutton Park. In November 1885 Joshua Hodgetts was fined £5 and costs for opening the inn during prohibited hours; he had pleaded guilty, explaining that he was with friends 'having a conversation on political matters and the time slipped away before he was aware of it.' [110] Joshua Hodgetts failed to pay the poor rate in 1889, and in February 1892 was declared bankrupt. Though no longer landlord of the Greyhound, he remained in lodgings there.

In September 1898 the licensee was Jesse Hope who changed the name to Ye Olde Greyhound Inn and informed potential customers that he offered stables, accommodation for bicycles and for charabancs and other vehicles on private land. If this wasn't enough, he declared that the inn was 'situate in the centre of charming surroundings and with close proximity to Powell's Pool entrance to Sutton Park.' [111]   The relaunch clearly wasn't a great success because in 1906 the licence was held by William May. He had the misfortune to be' knocked down … and severely injured about the head' by John Page, who, with his companions, refused to leave when asked. Page was fined 10s with costs and three others were fined £1 with costs for refusing to leave.

The Halfway House

This public house took its name from the fact that it was halfway between Lichfield and Birmingham. For a time in the nineteenth century, however, it was also known as the New Inn. In 1861 the licensee was John Leader. In 1871 it was Thomas Whearing, who was also a farmer. In 1881 it was George Hastilow. In December 1886 he was fined 5s including costs for being drunk in charge of a horse and cart. In June 1887 Hastilow was seen by a police constable

---

[110] *Warwickshire Herald,* 19 November 1885.
[111] *Harborne Herald,* 3 September 1898

'wrestling' with his wife in the kitchen; he was said to be 'very drunk' and fined 10s with costs. [112] Hastilow died of bronchitis in May 1888 and was succeeded by his wife Elizabeth.

The Horse and Jockey

Situated at the end of the turnpike road that began at the White Swan in West Bromwich and on the turnpike road that ran from Birmingham into Sutton, the Horse and Jockey was able to attract a good deal of custom from those visiting Sutton. Many of these visitors came to watch horse races – hence the name of the inn. The first proprietor of the Horse and Jockey was Stephen Ireland, who in 1781 began brewing and selling beer at his cottage. [113]

It is not clear who took over from Ireland, but in 1824 the owner put the inn up for sale by private contract because he was 'entering into the manufacturing business.' [114] The freehold was owned by the corporation. The purchaser of the house and the lease was Joseph Howard who had been a shopkeeper and publican in Wishaw. The advertisement placed in a Birmingham newspaper tells us that at this time the Horse and Jockey consisted of a large front and back room, a tap room, a kitchen and five bedrooms. Outside was a yard and provision for keeping cows and pigs, as well as a 'capital kitchen garden, about a quarter of an acre, well planted and stocked with choice fruit trees.' [115] The annual rent for the kitchen garden was £20; Howard was also offered the opportunity to rent another 10-50 acres of arable and pasture land but we do not know if he decided to do this. Like so many inn-keepers at this time, Howard was also involved in small-scale farming. He was no longer the proprietor of the inn at the time of his death in 1834.

Auctions were frequently held at the Horse and Jockey. In April 1825 the lots included brewing vessels, furniture, a fishing net 20

---

[112] *Birmingham Suburban Times,* 4 June 1887.
[113] See schlhrg.org.uk/history-spot/101-articles-1-40/1875-horse-jockey-34.html
[114] *Aris's Birmingham Gazette,* 6 September 1824.
[115] Ibid.

yards long and an 'excellent duck gun.' [116] In October 1828 freehold land and buildings fronting the turnpike road from Birmingham brought in a decent-sized crowd. There would be a sizeable auction of livestock at the Trinity Fair, which had taken place for centuries in the town. In June 1871 waiting to be sold were 'well-bred steers, barren stirks, capital new milch cows, 150 fat and store sheep and seven strong store pigs.' [117] The tenants of the inn themselves often had animals for sale. In 1864 a Brittany cow with her second calf was for sale at £12; and in June 1866 a sow and two pigs and two sows in pig were available. An advertisement was placed in a Birmingham paper in 1866 stating that, 'The large pig that was balloted for at the Horse and Jockey, Maney, Sutton Coldfield, to be seen dead this day (Wednesday).' [118]

The clientele of the Horse and Jockey were for the most part working men. Some might spend many hours there on 'a loose day.' [119] Inevitably there were from time-to-time outbreaks of disorderly behaviour. In July 1858 William Greaves became involved in a fight with two other men and received a black eye. What made this a widely-talked about incident locally was that Greaves was a police constable who had called in the Horse and Jockey after spending several hours giving evidence at the Petty Sessions in Sutton. He was suspended from his duties and the magistrates declared his conduct to be 'very disgraceful.' [120] During his eight months as a police constable Greaves had conducted himself well and so the magistrates decided that 'they should put a light punishment on him' by imposing a fine of 5s with costs of 13s 6d. In July 1882 Charles Cook, a labourer from Erdington, visited the inn and proceeded to bite off part of the tail of a friend's dog. He claimed that he had been given permission to do this – which was denied - and that he 'had

---

[116] Ibid., 18 April 1825.

[117] *Aris's Birmingham Gazette,* 3 June 1871.

[118] *Birmingham Daily Post,* 17 January 1866. There had been a lottery for the pig

[119] *Birmingham Journal,* 31 July 1858.

[120] Ibid.

bitten hundreds of dogs' tails off and that they used to be brought to him from long distances for that purpose.' [121] This defence did Cook no good at all: magistrates decided that he had behaved with wanton cruelty and fined him 10s including costs. In May 1906 two Birmingham men Arthur Godfrey and Edward Baxter refused to pay for a broken glass and then refused to leave when asked. When a police constable was called, they informed him that 'he had no business in the house and said they would go to the police station and see the matter out but, when they had only gone half way, they changed their minds.' The magistrates fined them 17s 6d each which included costs and part of the prosecuting solicitor's fee.

The Horse And Jockey, 1892

In the third quarter of the nineteenth century Thomas Bond was the licensee of the Horse and Jockey. When he died in 1886, the licence was transferred to his wife Caroline Bond. Within a year she had left and in quick succession a Mr Williams, Richard Turner and Mrs Shaw (whose late husband had kept the Wylde Green Hotel) held the

---

[121] *Birmingham Mail,* 5 July 1882.

licence. At the beginning of the twentieth century the inn was being run by Frederick Wilson and his wife Maud. Wilson kept four heifers at Stonnall and in March 1905 was fined for denying them food so that they 'were hardly able to walk.' [122] With the departure of the Wilsons, the new owner installed a manager Leonard Barlow, who had previously been head barman at St. James' Restaurant in New Street, Birmingham. The inn regularly advertised for young people to fill such positions as bar-potman, who was expected to live in, or as the custodian of the horse and trap and to 'make himself generally useful.' [123]

The lease of the Horse and Jockey was acquired by Ansells. In 1906 the brewery decided to rebuild the inn. A resident of Jockey Road was impressed: 'Suppose Messrs. Ansells, instead of studying the neighbourhood, had built it in the gin-palace style, it would have been a standing eyesore for years. They are to be congratulated for not doing so and for allowing their architect full scope for his artistic ability and originality.' [124] In March 1910 Ansells applied for permission to build a dining room with dimensions of 18' by 36'. 'Considerable business was done owing to people coming from the trams', it was argued; regarded as 'a high class' public house, permission was given. [125] At this time the licensee was James Walker.

The King's Arms

At the turn of the twentieth century, patrons of the King's Arms were able to visit a nursery next door where a dozen violas could be had for 2s and a dozen chrysanthemums for 3s. The licensees of the King's Arms in the 1880s were William Hughes and then his wife Annie, who were followed by Frank Wakefield – who moved to the Old Dog - and then by William Law. In October 1894 Law put one of his horses up for sale, which he described as 'free and fast in

---

[122] *Birmingham Daily Gazette,* 9 March 1905.
[123] *Birmingham Mail,* 7 August 1914.
[124] Ibid., 9 July 1906.
[125] Ibid., 9 March 1910.

harness, sound and passes steam'; in December 1897 he was advertising for a boy to look after a pony and 'make himself generally useful.' [126]   Then came Henry Sackeld and Thomas Pearson, with the nursery as their neighbours.

For both Sackeld and Pearson running the King's Arms proved disastrous. Sackeld acquired the licence at the beginning of 1898, having never run a public house before. In March 1900 he was fined 5s for being drunk on the premises. This he attributed to 'my old woman' and declared that he would relinquish the inn and return to his former business. [127] With his departure, Pearson bought the lease and acquired the licence. He borrowed the £1,400 necessary to buy the lease from the Cape Money Society of Smethwick and purchased the stock and fittings himself for £500. [128] He had previously been licensee at the Roebuck Inn in Edgbaston. At first the tavern drew in enough customers, but Pearson's financial position deteriorated, with him losing the lease to Ansells and also attempting to buy the freehold. Pearson's liabilities amounted to £2,058 and his assets were 'practically nil.' [129] He was bankrupt. Pearson's successor was John Preston and he ran into trouble of a different sort. In April 1911 he was fined 10s with 13s 6d costs for watering down whiskey. He claimed that his charwoman must have been responsible.

There were arrests at the King's Arms. In January 1907 three men were caught with house-breaking equipment as they ate their dinner; two were sentenced to twelve months with hard labour and one to three months with hard labour. In October 1909 Francis Hall stole a silver watch and money from his landlord. When he was arrested at the King's Arms, he was seeking to conceal these articles by 'wearing three pairs of pants and two shirts.' [130]

---

[126] *Birmingham Daily Post,* 8 October 1894, 17 December 1897.

[127] *Harborne Herald,* 17 March 1900.

[128] For the Cape Money Society see *Birmingham Daily Gazette,* 27 February 1907. At this point it was paying a dividend of 7% per £50 share per quarter.

[129] *Birmingham Mail,* 11 September 1905.

[130] *Birmingham Daily Gazette,* 11 October 1909.

The Museum Hotel

Opened in 1870, the Museum Hotel was situated on the corner of Park Road and the newly-christened Parade and was a few minutes' walk from the railway station. It sought to cater for middle class visitors to Sutton who arrived to take in the air of the park. It also had cheaper rooms for cyclists, and skilled working men could be found in the bar every evening. At first it was run by Thomas Webb, an experienced publican, and his wife, Mary. In December 1873 the hotel was put up for sale. It was described as 'very pleasantly situated … (with) compact premises, transacting a good trade.' [131] The asking price was £800.

The Museum Hotel, c.1888

In the early 1880s the ownership of the hotel was transferred to William Harrison, who was born in Birmingham in 1852. He was married to Maria and they had two young children. He was a member of the Brothers of the Buffalo Lodge, an organization similar to the Freemasons. When Harrison died in February 1886,

---

[131] *Birmingham Daily Post,* 5 December 1873.

aged 34, the licence was transferred to his wife, but she survived her husband by only four years. The licence appears to have been transferred to Oliver Pemberton before her death.

Harrison employed three servants – whose duties including work in the bar and the dining room - and an ostler. During Pemberton's time, the ostler was Charles Dangerfield. In July 1888 'for some unexplained reason', he climbed out of his bedroom window and onto the roof from which he fell forty feet into the yard. Apart from a wound on his thigh, he was uninjured. [132] If this strange event left Pemberton bewildered, he was less surprised when a few months earlier he had had to forcibly eject two men Henry Green and Robert Dempster who were picking up other customers' glasses, draining them and throwing them onto the floor. They also managed to break three panes of glass. They were each fined 10s with costs of 16s.

Pemberton moved on to become the licensee of a public house in Tamworth, but in August 1887 was declared bankrupt. The licensee in 1890 was J.L. Matthew. He saw a carpenter he had employed sentenced to six weeks' imprisonment with hard labour for stealing three florins from a bedroom. He soon departed, and in 1891 John Toy was the licensee. His daughter Gertrude worked as a bar maid and when John Harris, a jeweller, entered the bar in June 1891 'in a blustering way', she refused to serve him the two pints of Bass' ale he ordered. Harris was drunk and 'very violent' at the police station after his arrest. [133] He was fined 10s with 12s costs. In August 1893 a drunken George Bartlan, a brass founder. challenged Toy to a fight and swore at a police constable; he was fined 5s including costs.

In 1897 the Museum underwent extensive alterations and additions, and the next year the licence was transferred temporarily from Henry Archer to James Smith. The new licensee Harry Richards was determined to make a go of it, taking out a series of newspaper advertisements to make clear that the hotel was under new

---

[132] *Birmingham Mail,* 26 July 1888.
[133] *Warwickshire Herald,* 18 June 1891.

management (and able to serve chops and steaks 'at the shortest notice.') [134]   Formal social events were regularly put on – for example, a smoking concert in July 1901 for the tradesmen of Sutton at which £3. 0s. 5d. was collected for a fund for volunteers returning from the war in South Africa.   In 1911 the licensee of the Museum was Charles Dalman, married to Hannah and with two servants in residence, one of whom was his niece.

The New Road Tavern

Located in Hill, the New Road Tavern was occupied in 1861 by Samuel Hill, who was also a farmer. By the late 1880s the licensee was Henry Green who was succeeded in turn by George Atkins, Agnes Jones, William Richards and Thomas Millward. Dinners were put on. The Sutton Coldfield Ratepayers Association held a dinner there in March 1895, but Millward's application for an extension of one hour on that night was refused on the grounds that 'it was quite a country district and most of those who attended would have some distance to go home …'[135]

In June 1894 'a bother took place in the tap room.'[136] Six men began fighting, and Joseph Smith, a foreman platelayer, happened to be there. A glass was thrown at him by James Kirk, striking his right eye. He also received a second blow from an unknown assailant which cut his head. Appearing in court with his head bandaged, Smith maintained that he did not know Kirk. Convicted of common assault, Kirk was sentenced to one month in prison with hard labour.

The Old Sun

This public house, situated in Coleshill Street, dated back to the late eighteenth century. For several generations it was in the possession of the Aldridge family. [137] The owner for many years was John

---

[134] *Harborne Herald,* 10 June 1899.

[135] *Warwickshire Herald,* 14 March 1895.

[136] Ibid., 28 June 1894.

[137] See sclhrg.org.uk/history-spot-/104-articles-121-160/2015-old-sun-138.html
Also see sclhrg.org.uk/research/proceedings/145-volume-2/2273-volume-2-

Aldridge. He was clearly man of some means because he also owned a malthouse adjoining the beer house and houses in Coleshill Street and Church Hill. When the house was put up for auction in January 1841 it was described as occupying 'one of the best situations in the town for business, having a frontage of upwards of 70 feet and may, at a trifling expense, be converted into four excellent dwelling houses, with shops suitable for respectable tradesmen.' [138] The inn, however, did not find a buyer, and nor did it in February 1845 when it was again put up for auction. In November 1855 the house was again for sale by auction, and the particulars referred to a 'capital' club room, sitting room, parlour 'convenient' bedrooms, a brewhouse, a stable and a garden.[139] This time William Goodwin came forward to buy it, and, in February 1856, Aldridge's furniture, brewing equipment, carts and cucumber frames and other items were put up for auction.

The new licensee was William Betts, who, in March 1857, found himself in possession of a greyhound left by a customer. He benefitted from gigs bringing visitors from Birmingham on Sunday afternoons for 'a fashionable break' and returning from outside the Old Sun at 7pm. [140] Betts was described by Richard Holbeche, a member of a prominent Sutton family, as 'a very popular host … his house was a great meeting place for Birmingham tradesmen who on Sundays drove their wives in gay bonnets to take the Sutton air. They came in smart dog-carts drawn by fast-trotting ponies …'[141] Sarah Holbeche, who kept a journal of local and family events, recorded that Betts 'died in consequence of an accident.' [142]

---

article-6-the-old-sun-public-house.html This short essay by Kate Kendall provides as full a list as it is possible to make of the licensees of the Old Sun.
[138] *Aris's Birmingham Gazette,* 4 January 1841.
[139] *Birmingham Journal,* 1856.
[140] *Birmingham Daily Post,* 2 June 1859.
[141] sclhrg.org.uk/images/stories/transcriptions/My-Recollections-of-Sutton Coldfield.pdf This account has been transcribed by Janet Jordan.
[142] sclhrg.org.uk/sarah-holbeche-diary.html?start=55

In the early 1870s William Goodwin's son Joseph had inherited the Old Sun. Henry Foden held the licence, but by 1873 he was dead and his wife Maria was landlady. That year, however, with her liabilities amounting to £478 6s 1d and assets to £57, she departed. Two years later the house was bought by Thomas Holbeche; Charles Kemp was the licensee. Because of ill health Holbeche made two attempts to sell the Old Sun in 1878. 'Under good management and judicious alterations this house would be the best in Sutton', the advertisement proclaimed. [143] Unfortunately this did persuade anyone to pay the sum Holbeche wanted and he remained the owner. In 1881 the licensee was James Pittham who lived there with his wife and two sons The two young men did not enter trades but assisted their father. Like at many of these houses, there was a single servant.

A Mrs Duncalfe was managing the house in October 1889 when one of her servants attempted to poison herself because 'she "fancied" some young man and he did not return it.' [144] She survived the attempt and Duncalfe welcomed her back to the Old Sun. In the 1890s the licensees were Frederick Careless, Allen Gunnell and Edwin Martin. There seems to have been little trouble at this tavern. The only incident of note occurred in May 1899 when John Peak, a carpenter accompanied by his wife, became embroiled in an argument with another customer. The two men went outside to fight, and Peak's wife 'fainted and fell, her dress being covered with mud.' [145] Peak was fined 2s 6d with 11s 6d costs. For a short time before the First World War the house was known by the unfortunate name of Ye Old Sun Inn. The Old Sun was demolished in 1938.

The Park Tavern

The Park Tavern – so called because it was situated directly opposite the entrance to Sutton Park at Four Oaks - was definitely in existence in the 1840s. The Park Tavern offered accommodation – in May

---

[143] Ibid., 19 August 1878.
[144] Ibid., 26 October 1889.
[145] *Warwickshire Herald,* 25 May 1899.

1869 an advertisement was placed in the newspapers offering a sitting room and two bedrooms. At the end of the nineteenth century there was a rapid turnover of licensees: Henry Jackson, Joseph Lamb, Henry Bowen, William Seedhouse, Joseph Russell and Maria Rose. In December 1882 Jackson sold a horse to Thomas Wilcox, a jeweller for 50 guineas. The horse proved to have several defects and the matter found its way to court. It was agreed to let Jackson keep the 50 guineas in exchange for Wilcox being able to have his choice from several others that Jackson owned. In October 1892 James Pickerell, a labourer, admitted being inebriated on the premises, even though he had only drunk ginger beer; he was fined 1s with costs. Joseph Russell clearly had the personality to be an engaging landlord; in later life he became a travelling entertainer, presumably performing in public houses.

By 1894 a Mrs Waits was the licensee. She employed George Trainor as an ostler. He removed eight young thrushes from nests in the garden and brought them into the tavern. They were 'young birds and could not peck.' [146] Trainor was fined costs of 7s and given a warning; the birds were let loose in Sutton Park. Waits also employed James Salt as a groom; in July 1895 he was fined 2s 6d with costs of 14s 6d for assaulting a customer. Thomas Shillock became the next licensee and his wife Emma carried on the business after his death; her brother worked for a time as a barman. By this time the tavern was describing itself as a hotel. In 1911 the licensee was Minton Toddington.

The Plough And Harrow

The Plough and Harrow was a beer house – it was refused a full licence as late as 1911 – and was situated at Muffin's Den, Roughley. It opened in the 1850s, with Mary Wallin as landlady. [147] The Plough and Harrow was visited chiefly by farmers and farm labourers. Its

---

[146] Ibid., 21 June 1894.
[147] See sclhrg.org.uk/history-spot/110-articles-361-400/1802-polugh-and-harrow-399.html

role in serving an agricultural area was evident when, in March 1885, an auction was held there of 'thirty Shropshire sheep, two two-year old steers, three good working cart horses, fourteen Tamworth pigs and a useful assortment of agricultural instruments … Also at the same time will be offered five down-calving Kerry heifers, in calf cow, a barren heifer and nine shorthorn stirks.' [148] When a young man was sought to work at the house in 1908, it was made clear in the advertisement that he should be 'one used to country work.' [149] No clubs met at the Plough and Harrow and no dinners were held there.

Mary Wallin was succeeded as licensee by Joseph Newbold who, in 1885, was succeeded by her son Joseph. However, he did hold the licence for long. In 1894 the licence was transferred from a widow F.E. Burton to James Clark. By the early twentieth century the beer house was in need of significant repair: in February 1907 the licence of the Plough and Harrow was not renewed on the grounds of it 'being insanitary and structurally unsuitable for a public house.' [150]

Improvements must have been made because the licence was renewed and the Plough and Harrow was soon advertising apartments for gentlemen or married couples. In the years before the First World War the landlord was Benjamin Scattergood who ran the house 'in a very respectable way.' [151] In September 1908 Scattergood's wife Mary Ann was killed when, during a spell of dizziness, she fell from a bedroom window. Scattergood tried to improve his house. In March 1910 he sought a music licence. The local branch of the British Women's Temperance Association protested that 'it was not for the well-being of the neighbourhood' but the magistrates dismissed their arguments as 'not very forcible' and the licence was granted.' [152] The B.W.T.A. were there again to

---

[148] *Warwickshire Herald,* 21 March 1885.
[149] *Birmingham Mail,* 26 October 1908.
[150] *Birmingham Daily Gazette,* 13 February 1907.
[151] *Birmingham Mail,* 7 March 1911.
[152] *Birmingham Daily Gazette,* 9 March 1910.

object to Scattergood's application for a full licence in March 1911. It declared that granting such a licence 'would only provide additional temptation for the women and girls of the district.' [153] This time they prevailed.

The Railway Inn

As the name suggests, the Railway Inn began business as a result of the opening of the railway line from Birmingham to Sutton in June 1862. There was a great increase in the number of people spending time in Sutton, and these visitors needed refreshments and, in some cases, overnight accommodation. The Railway Inn was located in Station Street, and, in 1871 the licensee was Thomas Taylor and his daughter was the housekeeper. In the 1880s, the proprietor was John Rochford. When the tenancy of his yard and stables by W. Allport came to an end in 1886, he had the area completely reconstructed so that he was able to 'offer accommodation for any number of horses and vehicles; good lock-up loose boxes suitable for racehorses; also extensive lock-up coach houses suitable for bicycle and tricycle clubs.' [154] There was also an 'excellent green for dancing.' [155]

Rochford succeeded in attracting the customers he sought. The Oddfellows met regularly at his inn, from where, once a year, they left in a procession headed by a brass band to a nearby field to engage in various sports.[156] In October 1887 what was called a potato show was held in buildings at the back of the inn – though no one minded if turnips and cabbages were also displayed. There was a prize for the heaviest potato. To Rochford's great satisfaction fifty men, including councillors, afterwards sat down to dinner. He was doubtless also very satisfied when, in February 1886, magistrates dismissed a police prosecution for keeping his house open during

---

[153] *Birmingham Mail,* 7 March 1911.
[154] *Birmingham Suburban Times,* 26 June 1886.
[155] Ibid.
[156] See ibid., 11 July 1885. The prizes for the winners of the sporting competitions included a clock, five cwt of coal, joints of meat and a plum pudding.

prohibited hours on the grounds that the six men drinking beer were his guests.

In November 1890 the licence of the Railway Inn was transferred from Alfred Millard to Samuel Clarke. When the licensee of the Old Dog Thomas Good was charged with permitting betting on his premises in November 1891, two of Clarke's customers had a bet for £10 that he had informed the police. Clarke died in November 1892 and his wife Mary became the licensee. She became involved with an unidentified man and became pregnant. Anxious about losing her business, Clarke sought the help of Elizabeth Wallis of Aston, who described herself a dressmaker and midwife. Wallis paid several visits to the Railway Inn and, at the end of October 1893, carried out an abortion. As a result of this, Clarke died. Wallis declared that she visited Clarke 'to help the "poor thing" out of her trouble and that all she did was only as a friend.' [157] The police searched her house in Aston and concluded that it 'had been largely used as one of immoral character.' [158] At the Assizes in Warwick in December 1893, Wallis faced a charge of wilful murder. The opinion of doctors was that Clarke had died of peritonitis as a result of the abortion. It took the jury 22 minutes to decide that Wallis did not intend to harm Clarke and was guilty of manslaughter. She was sentenced to eight years in prison. 'I did not do it', cried a tearful Wallis as she heard the sentence. [159]

In the early twentieth century Phillip Baggs and a Mr Satterthwaite were the landlords at the Railway Inn. In August 1909 Satterthwaite's son was heavily fined after he punched Louis Ellery at the Duke Inn and damaged his bicycle by throwing it across the road. Satterthwaite had believed – mistakenly – that Ellery was making advances to his wife.

---

[157] *Birmingham and Aston Chronicle,* 18 November 1893.
[158] Ibid., 11 November 1893,
[159] *Birmingham Daily Post,* 15 December 1893.

The Red Lion

In the eighteenth and early nineteenth centuries this inn played quite an important role in the affairs of Sutton. Auctions were held there – for example, of a freehold estate of 78 acres in Aston and Saltley in October 1801. The trustees of the turnpike road from Birmingham to Shenstone also met there. Meetings began at 11 am and to ensure they did not drag on, it was made clear that dinner would be on the table at precisely 2 pm. In May 1809 the trustees met at the inn to select a new surveyor. At this point the landlord was Daniel Aston. According to the Sutton diarist Sarah Holbeche, the inn 'became extinct' in 1813, when a Mr Carver kept the establishment. [160]

The Royal Oak

The Royal Oak, built in the 1860s, was to be found in Mill Street. The first licensee was Thomas Archer who was succeeded by his wife Elizabeth. [161] The building survived little more than twenty years before being pulled down by its owners the Lichfield Brewing Company in 1889.

A year later the Royal Oak Hotel opened on the site. Though this was intended to be a more respectable establishment than its predecessor, it was still possible to take dogs into the bar; in July 1891 a customer offered a reward when his dog Jerry disappeared. In 1892 Robert Hill held the licence; he sought to recruit a servant, offering accommodation and wages amounting annually to £13.

In 1893 the licence was transferred from W.E. Webster to Thomas Townsend and in 1894 to Thomas Robinson. The new landlord took out newspaper advertisements stressing that the hotel was under new management. Clubs began to meet at the Royal Oak – the local hockey club held a smoking party there in May 1900 and the arrival of one of their members who had volunteered to fight in the Boer

---

[160] schlhrg.org.uk/sarah-holbeche-diary.html?start+5

[161] See schlhrg.org.uk/history-spot/106-articles-201-240/2076-royal-oak-1880-amp-1920-204.html Also see schlhrg.org.uk/research/143-proceedings/volume-1/2255-the-royal-oak.html

War 'was the cause of an enthusiastic demonstration and the proceedings were brought to a close by the singing of a number of patriotic hymns.' [162] The hotel became the headquarters of the Sutton branch of the Aston Harriers, and by 1914 there was even a football club of young men calling itself Eversleigh F.C.

The Royal Oak, 1887

Of course the hotel had visitors it did not want. In summer 1895 a police constable was called to eject Catherine Murphy, who was drunk. She clearly lived a hard life. She informed the magistrates – as she had apparently done before – that her husband was threatening to beat her; 'an old offender', she received 14 days with hard labour. [163] In summer 1895 John Mason was ejected for being drunk and, when he was refused re-admission, used bad language; he was fined 5s with costs. In August 1906 William Roman, from a middle-class Sutton family, organized a betting syndicate in an outhouse at the hotel. He denied handing out betting slips, and could offer no

---

162 *Birmingham Daily Post,* 7 May 1900.
163 *Warwickshire Herald,* 1 August 1895.

explanation for evidence presented to him that he had. The magistrates expressed their dismay at his 'swearing lies' and fined him £3 with costs.[164]

The Station

There appear to have been very few incidents of drunken and disorderly behaviour at the Station. In 1865 it was advertising apartments with board for gentlemen at 30s a week, and it was soon styling itself the Station Hotel. It sought to attract clubs – a lodge of freemasons and the organisers of the Sutton and District League met there. In September 1883, after a friendly shooting competition at the rifle range in Sutton Park, ten members of No. 7 Company 1st Warwickshire and ten members of the Sutton Company 1st Staffordshire were treated to 'a most welcome repast' at the Station by one of the officers. [165]

In July 1865 the new landlady Mrs Richards – formerly of the Hen and Chickens Hotel in Birmingham – arranged a house-warming dinner at the Station. Guests paid 5s and dinner was 'on the table at five o'clock to the minute.' [166] Shortly before the event Richards had advertised for a waitress and 'a steady woman as cook'; the cook either left or wasn't satisfactory because a few months afterwards she was advertising for 'a plain cook; must know her business.' [167]

In 1871 and 1881 the licensees were, respectively, George Jones and William Stent; both men were assisted by their wives and a barmaid who lived in. By the middle of 1880s the licence was held by Henry

---

[164] *Birmingham Mail,* 21 August 1906. There was also a public house called the Royal Oak in Streetly. It was better known as the Parson and Clerk in consequence of a long-running and bitter dispute in the late eighteenth century between John Gough of Perry Hall and Thomas Lane, the rector of Handsworth. It is said Gough mocked Lane by placing a depiction on the roof of the Royal Oak of a parson bowed in prayer in the company of a clerk wielding an axe See G. Stunt, *Perry Hall Yesterdays* (Barr & Aston Local History Society, 2016), pp. 70-1.
[165] Ibid., 17 September 1883.
[166] *Birmingham Daily Post,* 13 July 1865.
[167] Ibid., 23 May, 18 September 1865.

Mitchell, and the house was owned by his brewery. [168] A pint of mild could be had for 4d. In 1890 the licence was transferred from John Williams to John Wright. Immediately before the First World War the Station had a manager, George Short, who lived there with his wife, a barmaid and a servant.

The Sutton Park Inn

In the census of 1861 the occupant of this public house saw himself, first and foremost, as a farmer – and then as a licensed victualler. Boldmere at this time was referred to as a village, and there were not enough people living there for the holder of the licence to make enough money to survive on. However, in the years which followed, with an influx of day trippers, the house was able to exploit its proximity to Sutton Park. Richard Osman, the licensee in the 1880s and 1890s, was certainly not a farmer. He was in fact supplementing his income from the inn by manufacturing mineral water at a small factory in Jockey Lane. This he sold at the Sutton Park Inn and tried to supply to other public houses in the town. His supply of water came from Sutton Park. There was a James Osman – presumably his brother – manufacturing mineral water in Birmingham at this time. [169] Osman began employing William Welsh as manager of the Sutton Park Inn when he also acquired the licence to the Market Tavern, also in Boldmere, but this was seemingly a short-lived venture.

Yet, though the inn saw increased numbers of visitors, it remained at the heart of its community. The Boldmere Wake – an afternoon of sporting events - took place in a field near the inn. 'All events were well contested and created much amusement', it was reported, 'especially the married and single women's races and the donkey

---

[168] In 1893 shareholders in Henry Mitchell & Co. were paid a dividend of 8%.

[169] See *Birmingham Daily Post*, 26 February 1885. James Osman traded as the Birmingham Syphon Company.

races.' [170]   Afterwards many of those involved retired to the Sutton Park Inn The committee of the Boldmere and Wylde Green Flower Show, which was revived in 1893, met at the inn. At its show in August 1894, in the grounds of a private residence, flowers, vegetables and fruit were displayed in two tents. The first prize for a dish of potatoes was a five-pronged fork and the second prize, donated by Osman, was a bottle of whiskey.

The Boldmere Working Men's Association met at the Sutton Park Inn. Their annual dinner there in November 1892 'gave every satisfaction and, being of a substantial character, well cooked and served, reflected the greatest credit on Host and Mrs R. Osman.' [171] This association sought to ensure that the town council did not forget that there were working class residents in Sutton. There was a heated meeting in May 1896 to consider the intention of the town council to introduce charges for stallholders who sold refreshments in Sutton Park – the charge of 5s for a table 8' in length was declared to be 'very wrong, unjust and tyrannical … their rights and privileges were … (being) snatched away at a moment's notice.' [172]

The Swan

The Swan had stood at the north entrance to Sutton since the sixteenth century. It was mentioned favourably in the reminiscences of a journey made on foot through England by a young German called Karl Philipp Moritz in 1782: Moritz recorded that he stayed in Sutton inexpensively 'at a small inn with the sign of the Swan, under which was written Aulton, brickmaker. This seemed to have something in it that suited me …' [173]

---

[170] *Warwickshire Herald,* 10 October 1889. The prize for the married and single women's races were, respectively, 5s and 2s 6d. The men competed for casks of ale and a leg of mutton.
[171] Ibid., 17 November 1892,
[172] Ibid., 21 May 1896.
[173] sclhrg.org.uk/history-spot/105-articles-161-200/2051-top-swan-177.html

At the beginning of the nineteenth century the land on which the Swan stood was owned by Daniel Aulton. When he died at the end of 1825, the estate went to auction. As well as the inn, a large house, divided into two dwellings which included a shop, was also to be found on the site. There were stables for visitors to the inn, a 'well of good water and pump' and a garden 'proper for building upon.' [174] The landlord of the inn for over twenty years until his death at the age of 87 in December 1828 was Charles Spencer. He was succeeded by his niece Frances Roe in June 1829, but four years later she was dead.

In March 1840 the Swan was again up for sale. An inquest was held there for Charles Barker, the headmaster of Bishop Vesey's Grammar School, in October 1842 after he died whilst returning from Penns Hall in October 1842; the jury returned a verdict of 'dying by visitation of God.' [175] In April 1863 the licence was transferred from Thomas Reynolds to Peter M'Knight, who had been 'for upwards of ten years under-bailiff at the New College.' [176] The Swan was advertised for sale in early summer 1865: Sutton Park made the situation 'proverbially healthy' and the inn was 'now transacting a good and increasing business … the rapid improvement of the neighbourhood offers a rare opportunity of extending a profitable trade.' [177]

Then, unexpectedly, the Swan was the scene of great drama. In March 1870 Elizabeth Deakin, the wife of the licensee William Deakin, died at the inn in circumstances that remained a mystery; the verdict of the jury at the inquest, after many hours of deliberation, was that she 'died from wounds and bruises but how they were inflicted there was not sufficient evidence to show.' It is clear that Deakin and his wife did not get on. He was her second husband, and

---

[174] *Aris's Birmingham Gazette,* 30 January 1826.
[175] Ibid., 24 October 1842.
[176] *Birmingham Daily Gazette,* 2 April 1863. The New College of Preceptors was an educational institution in Birmingham.
[177] *Birmingham Daily Post,* 16 May 1865. See ibid., 20 May 1865 for the clearance of furniture, brewing utensils and the stock of ale, port and sherry.

her 16-year old son William Lovett lived with them. Deakin complained that his wife was a heavy drinker and a police constable reported that, on one occasion when she was lying intoxicated outside the inn, her husband 'refused to help get her in, saying that was the best place for her.' On the day that she sustained the injuries that led to her death Elizabeth claimed that her husband had struck her in the kitchen before leaving the premises; one witness claimed he saw Deakin also kick her and her face was reported to be badly swollen. When Deakin returned, he said he found his wife lying on the floor of the cellar. He claimed that she had fallen down the steps and went immediately in search of a police constable. A few days later Elizabeth died. [178]

William Lovett claimed that his step father was not in the habit of hitting his mother and that she was 'given to drinking and sometimes tumbled about and injured herself.' J.T. Smith, a local doctor, confirmed that he had been called to see Elizabeth when she was previously intoxicated and that the cause of death was most likely a fall down the cellar steps. The coroner informed Deakin that he had certainly mistreated his wife and narrowly escaped a verdict of murder or manslaughter. Local opinion certainly believed that the blame for his wife's death lay with Deakin: as he left the inquest he was 'rather roughly handled by an indignant crowd assembled outside.' [179]

To distinguish it from the Swan Hotel, the inn became known as the Top Swan. [180] In 1881 Alfred Ogden arrived as its tenant, paying £123 for the licence and fixtures. He had previously run the Ingleby Arms in Birmingham. The Top Swan was clearly a jolly place for a night-out. In August 1885 Ogden recruited a pianist for Saturday evenings. There was, however, still trouble for Ogden to deal with. In May 1885 Edward Wood and James Powell were sentenced to 21

---

[178] *Illustrated Midland News,* 9 April 1870.

[179] Ibid. Also see *Birmingham Daily Post,* 2 April 1870.

[180] For the Swan Hotel, previously known as the Railway Hotel and later as the Royal Hotel, see S, Roberts, *Glimpses into Sutton's Past Part II 1851-1885,* p. 61

days with hard labour for stealing a bottle of orange bitters – which was added to spirits - from the Top Swan; and in May 1889 Frank Nevill and David Johnson, both market gardeners, were fined 5s each with costs for refusing to leave when Ogden asked them to, with the magistrates declaring that they were 'as determined to protect the publicans as the public.' [181]

The Top Swan and neighbouring Bishop Vesey's Grammar School

Ogden found himself in hot water in February 1891. He was charged with selling adulterated rum. He argued that he was confined to bed by illness at the time and that it was probably his wife who was responsible. The magistrates declared this to be 'no excuse' and fined him 1s with 12s costs. [182] Ogden's troubles were only to get worse. In November 1892 the licence was transferred from Ogden to Henry James. This was because Ogden was deep in debt. In January 1893 it was revealed that his debts stood at £328 and his

---

181 *Birmingham Suburban Times,* 4 May 1889.
182 *Warwickshire Herald,* 5 February 1891.

assets at £7. His only creditors were the Lichfield Brewery Company, who held the lease and from whom he bought all his stock at a discount which he believed was too modest. An arrangement with the brewery to ease him out fell through, and Ogden sold the fixtures to the next tenant Henry James for £20. Ogden had not helped himself by failing to keep proper books of accounts. His discharge was suspended for two years.

By 1893 Edward Kelly was the landlord and the inn was up for sale. It was hardly a propitious start for Kelly when, in September 1893, he was fined 40s for selling ale to a customer who was already intoxicated. Within a few years George Walker was the landlord. He met William Sambrook at his inn, who already had 13 convictions to his name; he refused to leave and was fined 5s in February 1896. Frank Wakefield soon replaced Walker, and in February 1897 the Top Swan, 'now doing an excellent trade', was up for sale. [183]

The Boer War of 1899-1902 provoked strong feelings of patriotism across the country, but most especially in Birmingham where the local hero Joseph Chamberlain, as Colonial Secretary, was closely associated with it. There were, however, dissenting voices, one of which was Richard Clark, the licensee of the Swan. Clark made no secret of his opposition to the war. Inevitably this provoked a reaction. In the evening of 24 May 1899 a crowd estimated at 250-300 gathered outside the inn and began to throw stones at it. There were said to be cries of "throw up, lads" and "bang it in". [184] Clark was actually in Birmingham that evening – but his wife and mother were at the inn and it must have been a terrifying experience for them. Ernest Falconbridge, a plumber, and Charles Critchley, an errand boy, were charged with wilful damage to the Top Swan – which amounted to £7 15s - and William West, a baker, with aiding and abetting. Though West said of Clark that he would have liked 'to have seen him thrown into Blackroot Pool', he denied the charge

---

[183] *Harborne Herald,* 22 February 1897.
[184] *Birmingham Suburban Times,* 23 June 1900.

and claimed he went looking for a police constable. [185] All three were found guilty, Falconbridge and Clarke each being fined 2s 6d with costs and White 40s. The magistrates suggested that it might have been wiser if Clarke had kept his opinions to himself.

By this time the Top Swan was 'in a most filthy state.'[186] The freehold and leasehold were sold by Davenports to the town council and the inn was demolished. A new technical school opened on the site in 1904.

The Three Tuns

This famous inn, located in High Street, is central to the story of Sutton Coldfield. It was created in the eighteenth century, 'a peculiar construction' when two buildings became one, with a new frontage. [187] In the first half of the nineteenth century the inn served as the post office, the stopping point for coaches and a venue for auctions, political meetings and dinners. A description of the Three Tuns from 1842 tells us that it was a 'spacious and well-accustomed inn consisting of five parlours, with detached club room, fifteen bedrooms and two kitchens, brewhouse and spacious cellars, stabling for twenty-six horses and lock-up coach houses.' [188] A description from 1872 shows the development of the inn, with billiards, smoking, sitting and commercial rooms (which could be hired out) – and two Hanson cabs. At the beginning of the nineteenth century a Mr Waddington was the inn keeper. From 1810 until 1855 the owner of the Three Tuns was Harry Smith, also a farmer.

When the journalist Alexander Somerville visited Sutton in 1846, he stayed at the Three Tuns:

'Stranger, if you have any luggage with you, give it to the elderly lady at the Three Tuns. It is the head inn of Sutton; she will take care

---

[185] Ibid., 23 June 1900.

[186] *Harborne Herald,* 29 September 1900.

[187] *Birmingham Mail,* 9 February 1904. See sclhrg.org.uk/history-spot/102-articles-41-80/1936-three-tuns-54.html

[188] *Aris's Birmingham Gazette,* 31 January 1842.

of it for you and not let it be mingled with the coats, cloaks, bags, books, maps, theodolites, levels and other appurtenances of the Trent Valley branch railway surveyors. The room is sacred to them; the old lady says "master" ordered the room to be kept shut. Master is pleased that a railway is coming to Sutton and so master may. Where the artisans of Birmingham have come by the hundred to the meadows and wooded park, to the streamlets and the little lakes in the park of Sutton to recreate themselves, they will come by the thousand, wives and children with them, when they have a railway. Give the good lady everything but the walking stick and, with it in hand, let us out.' [189]

The auctioneers Henry Jacob of Birmingham and Solomon Smith and Samuel Kempson – both Sutton men - made frequent appearances at the Three Tuns. In November 1801 the house of Mrs Gamble, lately dead, was put up for auction. It was described as 'suitable for a large and genteel family' with 'excellent gardens in high condition and well planted.' [190] In November 1829 the trustees of the turnpike road that ran from Birmingham to Watford Gap arranged an auction of the Aston and Sutton toll gates. They made clear that the successful bids needed to match those of the previous year which had reached £1,800 each. Timber from Sutton Park or the Four Oaks estate could be inspected before an auction – in April 1830 men interested in the oak trees of Sir Edmund Hartopp's estate were invited to contact his gardener Thomas Clews. In May 1846 Kempson arranged an auction of his own 142-acre estate in Little Sutton, which included a family house 'handsomely fitted up with marble chimney pieces' and a farm house. [191]

When John Harris, the commissioner who supervised the implementation of enclosure in Sutton, arrived, he stayed at the

---

[189] *Manchester Times,* 20 November 1846. There were plans to build a railway line at this time which would have connected Birmingham with Sutton. In the event the line was not opened for another 16 years.
[190] *Aris's Birmingham Gazette,* 5 October 1801.
[191] Ibid., 4 May 1846

Three Tuns and held his meetings there. Enclosure in Sutton, as elsewhere, enabled landowners to expand their estates and deprived the poor of long-established rights of grazing stock and gathering fuel on the common land. It was also at the Three Tuns that the Sutton Coldfield Protection Society was established in 1849 by Edward Swynfen Parker Jervis of Little Aston Hall and other leading figures in the town alarmed by the repeal of the Corn Laws three years earlier. The manifesto of this protectionist body was rather alarming, predicting that free trade would lead to 'national ruin … (and) to the downfall of the Empire.' [192] Sutton Tories were later to use the Three Tuns as their headquarters during election campaigns in North Warwickshire.

Dinners were held in the club room. At the beginning of 1855 a dinner was held for two young men who were departing as officers for the Crimea; one of them, in his speech, declared to much laughter that he hoped 'the war would make them both colonels at least.' [193] In August 1859 over 200 employees of the Birmingham boot manufacturers Aaron & Noah were delivered to the Three Tuns in omnibuses where they enjoyed 'an excellent substantial dinner' followed by dancing in Sutton Park. [194]

E.M. Davis became the new proprietor of the Three Tuns in April 1856. The next month he held an opening dinner at the inn, the first course being served at exactly 3 pm. Within a few years he was gone, and James Davy had taken over. He promoted the inn as offering 'superior apartments for families and gentlemen', but also saw one of his servants sentenced to one month in prison for stealing money from the till. [195] Davy was followed by George Catlin, and a barmaid, a housemaid and a kitchen maid lived on the premises. Catlin owned a locally-celebrated pony called 'Little Wonder.' Early

---

[192] Ibid., 4 February 1850.
[193] Ibid., 13 February 1855.
[194] *Birmingham Daily Post,* 1 August 1859. These sort of 'treats' for employees were becoming increasingly common at this time.
[195] *Birmingham Daily Gazette,* 11 July 1863.

in 1872 he decided to sell 'Little Wonder', informing potential purchasers that the pony was 'warranted sound and perfectly quiet to ride and drive. Trots the rate of 16 miles an hour without whip.' [196]

The Three Tuns, 1870

The final decades of the nineteenth century saw a decline in the reputation of the Three Tuns. As a result of its good stabling, the inn continued to attract country people, but licensees came and went. In October 1885 Eliza Bridges was succeeded by Spencer Colman; in December 1888 H. Holden was on his way; in 1891 Henry Edwards died and his wife took over running the business; in May 1892 Clara Dohen was replaced by Clara Williams, who at the end of the year was succeeded by Richard Morris; in August 1895 Thomas Townsend was succeeded by Thomas Robinson; and in 1899 Ellen Soden was landlady.

The police constables often found themselves called to the Three Tuns. In May 1891 Richard Winder, a horse breaker, was fined 1s with 11s 6d costs for being drunk and refusing to leave the inn. In November 1892 he was back before the magistrates for exchanging

---

[196] *Birmingham Daily Post,* 17 February 1872.

blows with his friend Frederick Wilkins, a groom, at the inn and refusing a request from the barmaid to leave which resulted in both men being fined 1s with 10s 6d costs. In July 1899 Martin Panter put his hand through a window when a barmaid refused to serve him because he was drunk. This was his third offence of this nature and he was fined 5s 2d with costs. Unable to pay, he was sent to prison.

It was not just the customers who were breaking the law. In March 1903 the licensee Ellen Soden opened the inn on a Sunday afternoon and made no attempt to stop drunkenness. The fines and costs for her amounted to £13 2s. In the view of her convictions and the fact that the inn was 'unsuitable for the sale of intoxicating liquors and did not afford proper supervision' the police objected to the renewal of the licence in 1904.[197]

C.P. Hewlett, who succeeded Soden, managed to make improvements and the Three Tuns continued in business. It entered a billiards competition organized by local licensed victuallers in 1906; put on the annual dinner for the winter swimming club, whose season at Blackroot Pool ran from October to March, in 1907; and hosted a dog show at the end of 1914, at the end of which five dogs were auctioned and the proceeds donated to help Belgian refugees.

The White Horse

When the White Horse at Whitehouse Common was put up for sale in summer 1886, it was described as 'a capital, old licenced country inn, with old established business.' [198] We know that the licence holder in 1870 was Joseph James because that year his youngest daughter married the youngest son of John Willetts, landlord of the Old Dog. In the 1880s and into the 1890s the lease was held by Robert Lea, who also let a house he owned close to the White Lion. Lea was clearly not a man to be messed with, as Frederick Brown discovered when he 'strenuously refused' to leave the premises in June 1891. He smashed a quart jug and Lea forcibly removed him

---

197 *Birmingham Mail,* 9 February 1904.
198 *Birmingham Daily Post,* 18 June 1886.

from inn. [199] For this night-out Brown was fined 2s 6d for refusing to leave the house and 3s in damages for throwing a stone through a window after he was ejected. Lea believed it was important that the case had been brought forward to show him (Brown) and others that they could not do just as they liked on licenced premises.' [200]

The magistrates believed that Lea was a very good tenant. When he refused to serve a customer called Thomas Morgan who did not appear to be the traveller he claimed to be, the magistrates observed that Lea 'had behaved uncommonly well in the matter and … (was) to be commended.' [201] To be regarded as a bona fide traveller a customer had to be more than three miles from home; in this case Morgan 'admitted he "committed an error" at the White Horse, believing he was three miles from home.' [202]

Lea was followed as licensee by Emma Haskey. By this time the White Horse had become the headquarters of a Masonic lodge. On the day of their annual dinner, they would gather outside the inn at 9 am and walk in a procession to Holy Trinity for a service where, in June 1899, 'the musical part of the service was entered into with spirit, Mrs Eardley present on the organ.' They then returned to the inn for a 'bountiful repast' in a marquee, many of them comparing the quality of the food to that of a hotel. [203]

In the early years of the twentieth century Reuben Willetts held the licence. In December 1906 he served a pint of beer to William Mansell on condition that he did not share it with two other men in the house who he believed had drunk enough. Mansell placed his glass on the mantlepiece and the two men immediately drank it – followed by a second pint he bought, swearing he would drink it himself, and two bottles of beer he went and got from the Boot. The magistrates deemed this behaviour 'very reprehensible' and fined

---

[199] *Warwickshire Herald,* 18 June 1891.
[200] Ibid.
[201] *Warwickshire Herald,* 13 November 1890.
[202] Ibid., 13 November 1890.
[203] *Harborne Herald,* 1 July 1899.

Mansell 7s 6d. [204] Willetts learned that he should have ejected the two drunken men.

In February 1906 Samuel Runn was engaged as a plasterer when repairs were being undertaken at the White Horse. He had formerly held the licence for the Emmanuel College Arms. Whilst at the White Horse, he stole a jar containing two gallons of brandy. Despite 'a strong appeal for … lenient treatment', the magistrates fined him £5 including costs.[205]

The White Lion

The White Lion in Hill was in existence in the early part of the nineteenth century. Farm labourers made up a significant proportion of the local population. In 1861 the landlord was Edward Rochford. Subsequent landlords included John Walker, George Johnson, and Amelia Parker. Walker stayed only a few years at the White Lion before moving to the Crown in Four Oaks. A well-liked man 'of full habit of body', he 'fell like a log of wood' whilst watching military manoeuvres with friends at Watford Gap in October 1890; presumably he died of a heart attack. [206]

George Johnson found himself, in November 1889, charged on police evidence with the serious offence of selling alcohol to a man who was already drunk. Johnson denied that the man was inebriated and declared before the magistrates that 'he would supply him again if he asked for it.' [207] Fortunately for Johnson he had customers who confirmed that the man was not drunk and the case was dismissed.

Like others who ran public houses, Amelia Parker bred and sold pigs. She remained at the White Lion for eleven years, disposing of her licence to a brewery in 1906. The magistrates insisted she remained in place until a new tenant had been approved. Her decision to leave

---

[204] *Birmingham Mail,* 18 December 1906.

[205] *Birmingham Daily Gazette,*

[206] *Warwickshire Herald,* 6 November 1990.

[207] *Birmingham Daily Post,* 13 November 1889.

may have been influenced by a conviction – which was not identified in the newspapers - the previous year but thereafter the house had been 'well conducted.' [208]

The White Lion, c.1900

A new tenant was in place in 1907 after plans for minor structural alterations had been approved.

The Wylde Green Hotel

In the first half of the nineteenth century Wylde Green was agricultural land and sparsely populated. There was a farm, a scattering of houses and a small country house called Wylde Green House. There was no public house. But it was 'a beautiful situation to build a villa' and particularly after the opening of the railway line in 1862, with a station at Wylde Green, advertisements began to appear regularly in the newspapers offering 'eligible freehold building land.' [209] The Wylde Green Hotel was a product of these changing circumstances. Its situation on the main road from

---

[208] *Birmingham Mail,* 6 March 1906.
[209] *Aris's Birmingham Gazette,* 28 September 1840, 11 July 1863.

Birmingham, enabled it to draw in travellers in need of overnight accommodation. There were stables – some of them rented out – and an ostler was employed.

For a lengthy period James Shaw was the licence holder. In July 1878 he was nearly killed at New Street Station when he attempted to board a moving train and fell off the platform; for this act of recklessness he was fined in his absence 40s with costs. With his death in summer 1886, the licence was transferred to his wife Catherine. That autumn she sought to improve trade by opening a bowling green.

In summer 1889 a celebrity arrived to run the Wylde Green Hotel. He was John Page, a steeplechase jockey who had competed in the Grand National eleven times, winning in 1867 and 1872. He was married to Sarah; in September 1890 their 17-year old son, also John, died after a fall at Newmarket. [210] Sarah Page encouraged musicians to play outside the hotel. They would earn tips from customers and free ale from the landlady. When Lucy Gillett, a former servant whom she had known for a decade, was charged with stealing three rings and a comb from the bedroom of her new employer in Wylde Green, Sarah Page spoke up for her when she appeared before the magistrates, declaring 'although she had had diamond rings, brooches and other things lying about in her rooms, she had never missed anything.' [211] This testimony saved Gillett was from being sent to the Quarter Sessions at Warwick; Sarah Page paid the fine of £2.

In January 1895 the Wylde Green Hotel found itself at the centre of a food poisoning sensation. A large cauldron of soup, made of salted beef and vegetables, was prepared for the inhabitants of the area. There was no charge, and there was a large demand. Within hours those who drunk the soup began to suffer from vomiting and

---

[210] For obit. See *Birmingham Daily Post,* 11 June 1917.; also sites.google.com/site/allsoppfred/jockey/page-johnny
[211] *Warwickshire Herald,* 4 September 1890.

diarrhoea. It was reported that about 120 people succumbed, one of whom, a 47-year old woman Esther Ivens, died. A sample of the soup was sent to St. Bartholomew's Hospital in London and the report stated that it contained a considerable amount of bacteria. It was concluded that an outlet for sewage near where the soup was cooked was the cause of the outbreak. To their relief the Pages were exonerated. [212]

In 1898 Charles Adler succeeded John Page as the licence holder. [213] Alder had formerly held the licence at a pub in Aston without any concerns, but the magistrates had heard stories that the Wylde Green Hotel 'had not been conducted in a proper way': there was drunken behaviour and a fight outside the hotel for which William Wilson was fined 2s 6d with costs. [214] It was decided, however, that the fight could hardly be blamed on Alder.

There were other incidents of criminal behaviour. Clara Hands, a servant at the hotel, was prevented from playing cards and then assaulted by Henry Fellowes in May 1895; he was fined 13s 6d. In June 1911 a police constable who was watching the hotel 'in the interests of the licensee' refused entrance to Abe Tuckley who, in the ensuing struggle, threw a jug, hitting the constable in the face. As he was escorted to the police station, Tuckley 'was very violent and called upon the crowd for assistance.' The police constable was able to show the magistrates the bruises he had received from those who sided with Tuckley. For Tuckley the consequences of his behaviour were fines and costs amounting to 37s. [215]

---

[212] See S. Roberts, 'Gift of soup backfires', *Sutton Coldfield Chronicle,* 29 May 2021.
[213] Page died in June 1917 and was buried in the family grave at St. Michael's Church, Boldmere.
[214] *Warwickshire Herald,* 7 July 1898.
[215] *Birmingham Mail,* 6 June 1911.

ABOUT THE AUTHOR

Stephen Roberts holds honorary positions as Associate Professor at the Research School of Humanities and the Arts in the Australian National University and as a Senior Fellow at the Shakespeare Institute in the University of Birmingham. He has written extensively about Chartism and about Birmingham in the nineteenth century. A former reviews editor for *The Local Historian,* he now writes a weekly local history column for the *Sutton Coldfield Chronicle.*

The author engages in some vital research for this book

STUDIES OF SUTTON COLDFIELD

Glimpses into Sutton's Past Part I 1800-1850 (2020)

Glimpses into Sutton's Past Part II 1851-1885 (2021)

Glimpses into Sutton's Past Part III 1886-1914 (2021)

Glimpses into Sutton's Past: A Warwickshire Market Town 1800-1914 (2021).

Sutton Park 1900-1950: A Social History (2021)

BIRMINGHAM BIOGRAPHIES

Sir Benjamin Stone 1838-1914: Photographer, Traveller and Politician (2014)

Sir Richard Tangye 1833-1906: A Cornish Entrepreneur in Victorian Birmingham (2015)

Joseph Chamberlain's Highbury: A Very Public Private House (2015)

Joseph Gillott and Four Other Birmingham Manufacturers (2016),

Birmingham 1889: One Year in a Victorian City (2017)

Recollections of Victorian Birmingham (2018)

Webster & Horsfall & the Atlantic Cable (2020)

George Dawson & the Church of the Saviour (2020)